COUNSELING SKILLS FOR CHURCH LEADERSHIP

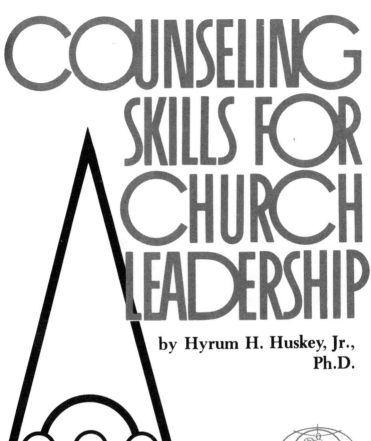

COUNSELING SKILLS FOR CHURCH LEADERSHIP

by Hyrum H. Huskey, Jr.,
Ph.D.

PASTORAL CARE OFFICE

HERALD
PUBLISHING HOUSE
Independence, Missouri

Library of Congress Cataloging in Publication Data

Huskey, Hyrum H.
  Counseling skills for church leadership.

  Bibliography: p.
  1. Pastoral counseling. I. Reorganized Church of Jesus Christ of Latter Day Saints. Pastoral Care Office.   II. Title.
BV4012.2.H85   253.5   80-20368
ISBN 0-8309-0295-3

Printed in the United States of America

CONTENTS

FOREWORD

The church has historically embraced the process of counseling as part of pastoral ministry. In a very real sense counseling can be viewed as a total *life-style* dedicated to wholistic living. Persons who live a counseling life-style are committed to a caring, loving, empathic way of life. The counseling process is simply one part of a larger framework of ministry that informs a person's feelings, thoughts, and actions.

Hyrum Huskey has written an introductory text that reflects the philosophy of counseling as a helping process, involving all people who live a pastoral ministry. He has provided the reader with a practical yet theoretically sound approach to developing helpful counseling skills. The book is divided into three parts: Foundations, Skills, and Professional Concerns. Each section has both theoretical and practical input, devoted to assisting the beginning counselor in concrete skill building.

As editor of the manuscript I found Hyrum to be deeply concerned and sensitive about providing a useful and enlightening resource for the church in the field of counseling. The Pastoral Care Office highly recommends this resource to all leaders of the church as they grow and develop in their counseling skills.

Harry J. Ashenhurst, Ph.D.

PART I

FOUNDATIONS

CHAPTER 1

THE CHURCH LEADER AS COUNSELOR

THE NATURE OF HELPING

Helping comes in many forms. Counseling another person is only one of many possible forms of helping. Other methods, among a multitude of possibilities, might include physical acts of kindness, charitable labor, or financial support. Even within the *verbal* helping process (or counseling) there are a number of levels at which the church leader might interact with someone experiencing the need for help.

At the lower end of the helping ladder is the concept of *instruction*. Instruction is common to many roles and is designed to provide information which is needed by larger groups of people. A church school teacher provides instruction to a class. The chairperson on a building committee might provide instruction concerning how the committee's future plans will be developed and carried out. These roles provide help to others in a general way. While instruction per se may not be "therapeutic" in intent, it is often more effective when the instructor makes use of good interpersonal

11

skills and a knowledge of the individual needs of those to whom the instruction is addressed.

The next step on the "helping ladder" is the use of *guidance* which is designed to meet the self direction and specific information needs of another person. It is the "fatherly advice" type of instruction which close friends or loved ones often use to add perspective to one another's ideas and concerns. It would be the kind of wisdom which a mother might pass on to her children. Guidance is a blend of instruction and counseling.

Many of the problems of everyday life—and particularly those which create unusual amounts of emotional stress—provide the opportunity for helping others through the process of *counseling.* Counseling is the process of helping to provide a secure relationship for another individual to use in exploring personal self concepts and in making the changes necessary to cope with the wide variety of problems which develop out of the normal crises of life. Crises which typically require counseling might include personal tragedy, sudden disruptive changes in one's normal environmental circumstances, values confusion, or simply an excessive amount of stress accumulated in a short period of time. Counseling is the helping process about which we will have more to say in this book. It is a role which, when properly approached, is well suited to the concerns of many persons who may seek advice and assistance.

Finally, there is *psychotherapy.* Psychotherapy is an advanced counseling or psychological process designed for helping people when major or incapacitating emotional problems are encountered. Often, extensive personality restructuring or carefully planned counseling therapy may be needed in order for individuals to successfully cope with their situations. The expertise required for dealing with such situations clearly calls for the church leader to make a referral to a psychiatrist, psychologist, clinical mental health counselor, or other helping professional with the advanced training to deal with severe forms of emotional disturbances. Procedures for making such referrals are outlined in chapter seven.

In spite of the varying purpose of these helping "levels," they all contain some common helping skills. These basic helping skills can be taught to and used by nearly all persons to improve their ability to communicate and relate effectively (therapeutically) with others. In this way, helping (in its broadest sense) is a function of all concerned human beings and is not limited solely to professional therapists. The key question which we, as potential "front-line" helpers, must ask ourselves is, "Am I the one who is trusted by this person and am I in a position to serve the needs of this person most effectively *at this time?*"

THE NEED FOR HELPING

A certain amount of stress is a natural part of our everyday life. We all need to generate some tension in order to be productive. Eliminating all challenges—and their accompanying stress—would make our lives very dull indeed! Too much stress, however, can result in excessive worry, anxiety, irritability, and confusion about how to cope with the confrontations encountered in the living process. It is under these conditions that the need for counseling often becomes apparent. All of us in the church need to be alert to the emotional needs of others and be ready to respond to such needs in a knowledgeable, caring, and concerned way. Persons in leadership roles, in particular, are often called upon to serve in the role of counselor.

At different points in our lives we may be living at different levels of stress. We may be in a panic and unable to cope at all with the demands made upon us by external circumstances. We may feel apathetic and simply be avoiding the responsibilities of life. We may be striving to meet the challenges of life and coping fairly well until some unforeseen event adds additional pressures and reduces our capacity to cope. Certainly, no one entirely escapes the stressful points in life's journey. Again and again the circumstances of living create the desire or need for some assistance. When such needs arise, we are often initially reluctant to seek the services of a professional counselor. At such points, it is natural to turn to those whom we trust and with whom we have experienced a special bond of fellowship. The church leader is a natural resource from whom to seek assistance, and such persons should be standing sources of hope and help for the emotionally burdened persons around them.

THE CHURCH LEADER AS HELPER

Long before the advent of this book and other helping resource aids, conscientious men and women in leadership positions have been serving in "counseling" roles to provide comfort and assistance to their fellow human beings. All of us are familiar with persons who seem to be natural helpers with many of the professional coun-

14

selor's skills already acquired in the process of living. Others, pressed into the counseling role, have proceeded in faith with limited skills and accomplished much in uplifting those around them. Nevertheless, such persons have often felt anxiety about their abilities to be effective helpers without the necessary formal training and education. Some have shied away from such a role altogether, questioning their "authority" for providing any counseling assistance whatsoever.

In spite of these limitations, church leaders can hardly avoid becoming involved in the multitude of daily entanglements and emotional crises which will be experienced by congregational members over their life-spans. Thus, we must recognize our responsibility to function as effective "first-stop" counselors to those whom we serve and with whom we interact. Helping skills are not the sole domain of professional therapists. Researchers and practitioners in the helping professions have repeatedly demonstrated that trained parapro-fessionals and volunteers have an important role to play in providing peer counseling assistance to the general public within natural social groups.

As a counselor or helping person you may simply provide a climate in which other persons can grow in their ability to meet their own emotional needs and requirements for personal growth. Some of this growth may require skilled professional assistance. Other opportunities can be provided by you. When the magic and mystery are taken away from the helping process, much help can still be provided by the average person who is willing to learn and practice the basic skills for effective interpersonal relations. For the church leader who does this, counseling will not simply be one of your roles; rather, it will become a way of life as you develop the rewarding capacity to help others at critical points in their lives.

RIGHTS AND RESPONSIBILITIES

Entering into any counseling relationship implies certain rights and responsibilities on your part as well as the part of your "client" (person seeking your assistance). These responsibilities are not to be taken lightly, since the expectations involved in their fulfillment will make up much of the substantive "method" in the counseling process.

As a counselor, you have the same rights any individual holds. You have the right to maintain personal autonomy in the relationship and to retain your own value system. You have the right to withdraw from any counseling relationship which you feel is harmful either to you or to the other person involved. Helpers also hold the prerogative of setting reasonable limits on their availability in terms of time expenditure, number of meeting times, and degree of involvement with clients outside the scheduled counseling times. Finally, you have the right to expect that persons seeking your assistance will eventually begin to assume some responsibility for their part in the relationship when they are capable of doing so.

As a helper you are also accountable for fulfilling the following major responsibilities:

1. To accept all persons in a positive, nonjudgmental way, maintaining a full belief in the client as a person of dignity and worth in God's sight.

16

2. To be aware of yourself and to be open to continued self growth as a person, capable of sharing yourself in appropriate ways with other persons.

3. To acquire training in helping skills suitable to the average level of helping involvements into which you intend to enter.

4. To allow all persons who seek your assistance the right to maintain their personal freedom and to make their own value decisions regarding their lives.

5. To maintain strict confidentiality concerning private matters discussed with you, and to assure that a client is never unwillingly identified with those concerns.

6. To be actively aware of other professional resources available in your community and to refer clients to such resources when their concerns or emotional status is beyond your capabilities as a helper.

7. To recognize and always act upon the fact that the helping relationship is designed to meet the needs of *the person seeking assistance* and not your needs.

All of the responsibilities listed above are actually the rights of the client. Persons seeking your assistance have the right to expect that you will fulfill these ethical obligations as a counseling helper. In addition, the client obviously has the same rights which you have as a person—freedom to accept or reject help and to limit the amount of time expended on the process of receiving help.

The person (client) seeking help also has the following responsibilities (which, unfortunately, are often overlooked):

1. For all self-choices and self-actions (we cannot assume another person's responsibility for self).

2. For either initiating or responding to the offer of help. In spite of our best efforts, many persons will reject counseling assistance and we who recognize their needs may be left to "weep over the people."

3. For contributing to the counseling relationship through the provision of information about the problem, appropriate self disclosure concerning the problem area, and a committed participation in the process of seeking solutions.

CHARACTERISTICS OF AN EFFECTIVE HELPER

Persons who sincerely seek to be effective helpers in the counseling encounter must be aware of certain personal attributes which are required of an effective helper, and seek to develop these ways of being in their own roles as a helper. Some of the desirable characteristics of helping persons include:

1. Recognizing that they are not perfect and gauging counseling "success" by how close they approach a goal—not assuming that they will always reach ideal results in every instance.

2. Striving to be aware of themselves and how others see them. This is an important first (and continuing!) step in the development of the capacity to be a helper to others.

3. Attempting to edify and encourage; avoiding unrealistic attitudes and expectations; avoiding the temptation to condemn.

4. Avoiding temptations to become *over*involved in ways which interfere with the ability to be a responsible

helper. Overinvolvement usually can be identified when counselors find themselves doing and saying things designed to meet their own desires and interests rather than the interests of their clients.

5. Recognizing that they are still in the process of self growth as counselors. Self love and love of others; self respect and respect for others; self confidence and confidence in others all tend to develop together.

6. Maintaining a basic trust and faith in people and the inner resources which the individual can develop and use to cope with his/her problems.

7. Maintaining a comfortable acceptance of helping intentions, including the avoidance of distortion and deception, facing unpleasant as well as pleasant times, and thinking in terms of possibilities rather than certainties.

8. Maintaining a sense of humor and ability to laugh at themselves.

9. Maintaining flexibility and the capacity to think in terms of varying perspectives.

10. Maintaining a high degree of tolerance for frustration and uncertainty (because there will be lots of both).

11. Recognizing and accepting their own limitations and making appropriate referrals if required.

12. Maintaining highly effective listening skills (see chapter three) and being capable of perceiving unstated feelings.

13. Being warm, genuine, and compassionate; recognizing that helping is more than just a role—it is a way of life.

14. Being open and self disclosing; allowing another person to know them as they are.

These then are the traits and attitudes which you will seek to develop in yourself if you wish to extend yourself effectively to others as a counselor. If you display these characteristics, your "authority" to act as an effective helper will not only be recognized—it will be utilized.

CHAPTER 2

THE HELPING PROCESS

"Helping another human being is basically a process of enabling that person to grow in the directions he (she) chooses—help should be defined mainly by the helpee. This means that the helpee not only selects the goals of his (her) own growth but that he (she) determines whether he (she) wants help at all."—Lawrence Brammer, *The Helping Relationship* (p. 3).

INTRODUCTORY COMMENTS

For several Sundays you have noticed that Mr. and Mrs. Jones either have not attended church or, when they have attended, have appeared withdrawn. You have just about decided to approach them and express your concern when Mrs. Jones, who attended alone today, comes up to you immediately following the service. In a hesitating, nervous voice she asks you, "May I see you in private for a few minutes? My husband and I are having a great deal of difficulty." (She begins to cry.)

The Smith family has been somewhat disrupted of late by the acting out behaviors of a teen-age son. Late one evening you receive an urgent phone call from Mr. Smith who informs you that this son has been picked up by the police for breaking into a construction shed.

Mr. Goodweather calls your home and asks if you could possibly meet him and Mrs. Goodweather after they return from work today. He sounds agitated and upset. As you stop by the Goodweather home after work, you learn that Mr. Goodweather's mother has cancer. Mr. Goodweather doesn't think he can handle "it."

As you learn of each of these circumstances, you sense the need to fulfill your role as a counselor. But how do you start the counseling process? What skills do you have that will be of help to these people? Should they be seen by a professional psychotherapist instead of you? What will happen in the helping process of counseling these persons who have sought you out? When persons need "counseling help" what is it that they are really asking for or need?

THE COUNSELING ENCOUNTER

As you become involved in attempting to counsel or help each of the persons who have sought you out for assistance, you also become involved in an "encounter" between two self systems: yours and that of the person with whom you are counseling. This relationship and its development is vital to the therapeutic process of helping another person through counseling. It is through this relationship that you can help to develop the inner resources of troubled persons and enable them to cope with the situations which face them.

This "encountering" process has both artistic and scientific aspects to it. It is "scientific" because it involves the application of skills which are measurable and have been researched to prove their effectiveness. It also involves maintaining an adequate knowledge base through study and self evaluation of successes and failures in working with others. However, no techniques or skills are sufficient without an active, artful participation by the counselor. Counselors must have the capacity to be aware of themselves and the operation of the Holy Spirit in their own lives. They must have the capacity to extend themselves to others in helpful ways. They must be intuitive in terms of the timing and nature of their responses and the application of their learned skills as counselors. They must be able to engender trust and confidence in others. In client-centered terms, this involves being "dependably real" as a person rather than "consistently rigid" in applying some technique of counseling.

The first requirement, then, in this "process" of counseling, is that you should be capable of developing your own self awareness and self acceptance. Your own "personhood" is the most effective tool in the counseling process and must be extended to another in a helpful way if the counseling encounter is to be successful. When you are capable of accepting your own self way of being in the world, and accept your own feelings in an authentic, responsible manner, you are then in a position to establish a counseling relationship which will be meaningful and helpful to a client.

The counselor's role is one of "facilitating" the process of growth in the other person. The relationship is the medium in which this is done. It is the "change agent" process through which the client's personal resources are mobilized to cope with the factors causing his or her emotional disturbance. The relationship is the medium through which the counselor recognizes and accepts other persons as they have the *potential to become.*

As the client and you move through this counseling encounter together, the client should be helped to change

FROM	TO
No sense of personal control	Making effective choices
Responsibility seen as external to self	Accepting personal responsibility for self
Hidden self needs and attitudes	An open, expressive self
Disowning personal feelings and meanings	Full ownership of personal meanings and feelings
Rigid personal constructs	Flexibility and openness to changing experience

24

FROM	TO
New actions based solely on past experience	New actions based on current understanding
Impersonal, distanced communication	Communicating with "I" statements
Vague self and spiritual awareness	Growing, expanded self and spiritual awareness
Irresponsibility, apathetic	Responsible; action-oriented

The counseling process and the counselor's role in it are designed to facilitate these changes.

STAGES IN THE COUNSELING PROCESS

We can visualize the counseling process as one in which the relationship is initiated and developed in a *facilitation* (or establishment) stage, is strengthened in a *transition* (or exploring) stage, and is finally fully used to aid in problem solving in the *action* (or working) stage. Each of these stages may last from one to many separate sessions with the client.

In the chart on page 26 these stages have been depicted in horizontal order from left to right at the top of the page. As the time spent in the counseling process increases, an *effective* counseling relationship should be evidenced by an accompanying increase in the quality and depth of the interpersonal interactions between the counselor and client. Also, the client's overall behavior pattern should be progressing toward the type of

THE COUNSELING PROCESS

Stages Major Concern Areas	Facilitation (establishment) Stage	Transition (exploring) Stage	Action (working) Stage
Process Orientation Focus	Trust; Safety; Rapport; "Being with"	Mutual acceptance; Exploring; Awareness; Confidence-building	Problem solving Integrating Independence Actualizing of realistic possibilities
Skill Dimensions	Listening Attending Empathy Warmth Respect	Concreteness Genuineness Self disclosure Immediacy	Confronting Decision making Goal setting Problem solving
Counselor's Work	Attending Reflecting Supporting Clarifying Summarizing Accepting	Focusing Structuring Modeling Interpreting Self disclosing	Confronting Intervening Mutual involvement Problem identi- fication
Client's Work	Accepting help Trusting Disclosing Permitting	Exploring Gaining self awareness Accepting self Confidence building	Assuming responsibility Integrating Choosing alter- natives Clarifying values Actualizing potentials
Self Changes	Disclosing	Exploring Awareness Acceptance Confidence	Integration Actualization
Spiritual Self Growth	Confused identity Seeking	Accepting spiritual self Feeling God's acceptance Reorienting Increased spiritual awareness Faith building	Reintegration of Spirit and self Utilization of potential (gifts) Extension of self for greater good Magnification of discipleship

Time Expended
———————————→
Quality of Interaction

activities shown in the third stage (problem solving, decision making, etc.).

It should be noted, however, that there is no definite moment when the counseling process progresses from one stage to another. At times the relationship will advance into a higher stage, only to fall back later as the client experiences a need to further explore a selected aspect of self. The counselor, too, may be moving within several of these stages in a single session with the client, aiding in a problem solution in one moment and strengthening the climate of trust in the next moment in order that a deeper problem may be approached and resolved.

In each of these "stages" of counseling, there are a number of "major concern areas." These are shown vertically on the accompanying chart and include the following:

1. The *process orientation (immediate) focus* of the process.

2. *Skill dimensions* involved at that stage of the process.

3. The *counselor's work* or primary task focus in that stage.

4. The *client's work* or most helpful task focus in that stage.

5. *Self changes* which should be taking place within the client's internal self structure system (and, it is hoped, to some degree in the counselor also).

6. *Spiritual self growth* changes which the client may be experiencing.

When the major concern areas are considered together with each stage of the counseling process, we can identify specific skills or tasks which are involved. These are shown vertically under each stage in the boxes on the chart. By considering the *major concern areas* and *task skills* of each stage, the counselor is provided with the direction and framework needed for understanding the ongoing process of counseling. The specific task skills will be discussed in more detail in chapters three through five. For now, we will simply outline the task skills within the three stages as they relate to the major concern areas of the counseling relationship.

THE FACILITATION STAGE

The facilitation stage is crucial to the initiation and maintenance of the counseling process. It is here that you must attempt to facilitate a workable relationship by establishing a climate of trust and safety for the person who is seeking your assistance. Establishing rapport with the client is a prerequisite and vital first step in building a productive counseling relationship. This rapport is built by your display of a genuine accepting, nonjudgmental attitude, and by your attempts to authentically "be with" and "confirm" the personhood of the client.

The work of establishing this type of relationship will be enhanced by your skill in listening to, attending to, showing warmth and empathy toward, and having a genuine respect for the other person with whom you are interacting. Your prime goal in this stage is simply to "be with" and follow the thoughts of the client by interacting and responding in a reflective, supporting manner to what is being said. As the counseling progresses, you may also wish to clarify and summarize some of the client's statements and understandings concerning the situation for which counseling has been sought.

The primary tasks of clients, in this stage, are to accept help, learn to trust the counselor's efforts, and permit themselves to be self disclosing to the degree that the counselor can begin to understand and operate within the clients' internal frames of reference. During this process, individuals will disclose something of their internal self structure systems (values, attitudes) to you, and both of you will gain a clearer picture of the clients' perceptions of the crisis situation.

The overall purpose of this first stage is to establish a meaningful, workable relationship between you and your client. You cannot simply express your acceptance of another person; that person must *feel* it! In this stage it is best (as it is throughout the counseling process) if the counselor can avoid overtalking, note-taking, restlessness, and similar behaviors and concentrate, instead, on listening to and fully understanding the client as a person. The immediate goal of counseling in this first stage is not to obtain a solution to all of the client's woes. Rather, it is to initiate and provide for the continuance of a needed helping process. Carkhuff and Berenson *(Beyond Counseling and Therapy*, pp. 153-154) have described this as a process of the client moving "downward and inward" as opposed to later stages of counseling when clients are normally better prepared to move "upward and outward." In short, this stage of the counseling process is best exemplified by the admonition of C. H. Patterson *(Relationship Counseling and Psychotherapy*, p. 116) that "counselors must be more concerned about *being someone* with the client than in *doing something to him.*"

THE TRANSITION STAGE

The transition or exploring stage might well be viewed as an advanced phase of the facilitation stage. As a basis of trust is developed between counselor and client, a climate of mutual acceptance and interpersonal confidence is established. In this climate, clients are able to explore all aspects of their self structures and increase their self awareness and options with regard to their current life space. This is a period in which clients, within the permissive acceptance of the counselor, can perform an in-depth reconnaissance of their self attitudes, feelings, and values. It is a time in which they should be helped to recognize and reaccept themselves *as they are* and as they *desire to be.* It is a time for exploring and personal reevaluation.

Specific task skills involved in this stage include the use of concreteness (being specific in the expression of feelings and experiences), genuineness (being "real"), personal self disclosure, and attempting to concentrate on the "here-and-now" aspects of the relationship (immediacy). You will use these skills yourself in order to help focus and structure the sessions toward client growth. You also use them to model growth-producing behaviors for the client. Clients use the same skills to further explore and accept themselves and to build confidence in self and confidence in the capacity of the counselor to be of help to them.

Ideally, the self structure system of the individual, at this stage, is one of increased openness. The observing

"I" self looks inward, exploring and accepting the "me" or *is*-ness of self. A new look at spiritual self aspects, too, is included in this increased self awareness and attitude of acceptance. Along with other aspects of self, there is an increased acceptance of the spiritual meanings and purposes of existence. One begins to feel more accepted by God and experiences an increased spiritual awareness on which to build his or her faith in ways which will enhance the person's ability to cope with stress more effectively.

THE ACTION STAGE

As the counseling relationship develops to its full potential as a helping process, clients are able to use their increased self awareness and acceptance of internal and external realities to clarify their true values, integrate various aspects and images within the self structure system, make responsible choices between alternatives, and actualize the realistic possibilities for improving the state of their lives. It is a time for reorientation of personal goals and behaviors and for assuming responsibility for their own lives and actions. With this assumption of a self responsible way of being in the world, a client also gains a renewed sense of independence, making goal setting, problem solving, and decision making easier and more self fulfilling. Thus, within the process described, a client is enabled to progress through a series of seven "R-word" states: *rapport* with another human being, *reconnaissance* of self, *recognizing* and *reaccepting* self, *reevaluation*, *reorientation* of goals and behaviors, and the acceptance of personal *responsibility* for change.

31

The counselor aids in this progress by actively intervening and being involved with the client in the problem solving and goal setting necessary to improve the client's life situation and outlook. The counselor has many roles to play in this stage as an attempt is made to identify and clarify the issues on which the client must work. You may be required to confront the client, actively but gently, when the client appears to be thinking or acting in a self destructive or irresponsible manner—thereby permitting and encouraging the client to make choices which are more appropriate or self enhancing with regard to his or her desired way of being.

The paraprofessional counselor must be careful, at this point, to stay within the bounds of his or her knowledge and expertise. Many problems will require the help of professional therapists or specialized agencies for proper handling and remediation. Still, there are many things which you can do to be of assistance and which may, in themselves, be sufficient. You can assist a client in identifying whether the real concerns are internal or external to themselves, thus clarifying whether the client must change or seek an environmental change. You can help the client identify which problems require immediate attention and which ones can be handled later. You can encourage the client to set realistic goals by helping him or her explore possible consequences of various types of actions. You can assist the client in determining whether feelings, things (events), or actions (self or others) are at the heart of the concerns. You can arrange "contracts" (written or verbal) with the client in order to encourage changes in behaviors or ways of feeling. Within your personal abilities and knowledge (which can always be expanded!), you can help clients learn needed skills such as being more assertive, learning better interpersonal skills, role-playing desired modes of living, and similar change-oriented activities. You can help identify which values are "real" for the client and which are "fantasy." And, finally, you can help clients manage conflicts and arrive at solutions to problems (see chapter five).

The self structure and self images of persons often change dramatically over the duration of the working stage of counseling. As clients begin to integrate *all* aspects of the self, rather than living lives focused on narrower perceptions or self interests, they are often able to actualize their real values, adopt new attitudes, and enhance their spiritual growth potential. They are better able to use talents and personal gifts in a manner which allows them to extend themselves to others in new and more productive ways. They may thereby promote the greater purposes of life and magnify their discipleship far beyond where they were prior to the event which precipitated the original need for counseling. Thus, opportunity is often born of crisis.

As the counseling process draws to a close—made unnecessary by the resolution of the original events which necessitated it—the problem of ending the counseling relationship arises. If the counseling relationship has been appropriately and successfully developed, termination is made easier by the client's increased sense of independence and success in handling his or her personal life. In fact, the most successful counseling encounters are marked by an ending in which clients feel that they changed themselves—which essentially is often true! Nevertheless, a bond of authentic personhood and Christian love will have grown between you and this other person and these bonds are difficult to end. The counselor's role is to encourage the client's sense of independence while assuring him or her that assistance and friendship are always there should they be needed in the future. This reassurance normally suffices and enables the formal counseling relationship to be ended until it is again needed.

THE RETURN OF INDIVIDUAL AUTONOMY

The end goal of all counseling relationships is to produce fully functional—or potentially fully functioning—persons who have successfully explored and clarified the various aspects of their lives and themselves. The higher self potentials will have been recognized and magnified through an increased recognition and acceptance of the responsibilities encompassed in discipleship. One precaution, however, is in order. The counselor must recognize that there is no shortcut to the counseling process. Too frequently, beginning counselors rush into the advanced stages of the counseling relationship without allowing the relationship itself to develop. Time for the client to gain the necessary increase in self awareness and self acceptance is not provided. Trust is not fully developed. While there is always a temptation to rush in with advice, and to get personal agony and suffering resolved quickly, you must develop the personal faith and capacity to withstand this temptation. Usually, clients have lived with their situation for some time anyway. There is simply no good shortcut to building an effective counseling relationship if the client's full potential as a person and a disciple is to be realized. Faith in self (and in God), like the grain of mustard seed, needs time to grow. The counseling process, properly nurtured and developed, provides that time.

PART II

SKILLS

CHAPTER 3

EFFECTIVE LISTENING

INTRODUCTORY COMMENTS ON SKILLS

The use of therapeutic communication skills is greatly enhanced if used in a meaningful framework or context such as provided in Part I of this book. Therefore, if you skipped the first two chapters to begin at this point, it is suggested that you return to read them before moving on. Learning and practicing the skills outlined in chapters three through five will then be much more meaningful.

There are three basic principles which should be followed for learning new skills. First, one must have a *knowledge* of the skill, including what it is and how it is used. Second, one must *practice* the skill in daily life and (in this case) in interactions with others. In this and the following two chapters, basic communication skills which are helpful to the counseling process will be discussed. Though these skills may appear to be rather simple and straightforward in nature, a great deal of practice is required to use them effectively. Practice exercises will be outlined so that you may practice the skill and examine your style in using it. Finally, you are encouraged to *further develop* and *use* the skills in your daily interactions with others and seek their feedback. In this way, you can make any necessary changes in your interpersonal style which you feel would improve your ability to be more helpful to clients during counseling.

At first, many of the skills will seem artificial or uncomfortable as you try to use them. The reason is that most of us are accustomed to *social* conversation rather than therapeutic communication. However, as you use and practice therapeutic ways of communicating, you will become more comfortable with this style of relating to others. Furthermore, most persons discover that their everyday relations with others also improve dramatically. Therapeutic communication opens the doors for persons to reach out and be themselves with you. This is an action which results in a good feeling for most people and one which they are seeking to experience. By acquiring good communication skills, you can be helpful to others both in and out of a "formal" counseling relationship.

LISTENING AS A HELPING TECHNIQUE

C. H. Patterson, a counseling psychologist at the University of Illinois, has stated (*Relationship Counseling and Psychotherapy*, p. 101) that "adhesive tape might be more useful than recording tape" for beginning counselors. Most inexperienced counselors spend too much time talking and not enough time *listening*. This is, in fact, a common problem even in everyday conversations between persons in social settings. Most of us would rather talk than listen. We spend most of the time, when another person is talking, thinking about what *we* will say next when our turn comes to speak! This is an ineffective listening habit.

Listening is an active process that requires hard work on the counselor's part. Yet active listening (giving full attention to the speaker) communicates to clients that you understand their experiences. Thus, active listening is almost always appreciated by the client. Still, paying *full* attention to something or someone is very difficult because we can usually think much faster than someone speaks. This means that our minds have "free time" to wander to other thoughts. You can experiment with your capacity to be fully attentive by trying the following exercise:

Exercise 1: **Pick a nearby object and concentrate on it for at least half a minute. Have someone keep time for you. Give the object your *full* attention and concentrate until your partner tells you the time is up. Discuss any difficulties which you had in trying to concentrate solely on this object. What other thoughts entered your mind?**

Most people find even this limited attention span difficult to maintain. They may think about whether the time is nearly up, what is on the next page of this book, or similar thoughts. Consider then how much effort is required to give someone your full attention when he or she is talking and stimulating a variety of thoughts in your own mind.

ATTENDING SKILLS IN LISTENING

What is really meant by the term "listening"? Is it something that is done only with our ears? Our ears plus our mind? Or more? Allen Ivey (*Basic Attending Skills,* Microtraining Participant Manual, p. 9) has used the term "attending behavior" to describe what it is that people *do* to help others know that "listening" is taking place. In other words, attending behaviors can make "listening" observable and demonstrate to clients that your attention is focused on them. This demonstration of attentiveness, in turn, encourages the client to continue talking about and exploring self.

Ivey (p. 9) describes attending behaviors in terms of
- eye contact,
- attentive body language, and
- verbal following.

These are further discussed in the following:

1. Eye contact: This simply means looking at the other person, particularly at the eyes. Probably more than anything else, eye contact demonstrates to other persons that they have your attention and interest. You may have had the experience of talking to someone who avoided looking at you. If so, you no doubt can recall the discomfort and nervousness that such action caused in you as a speaker.

Naturally, your eye contact should not be in the form of staring at the other person. Occasional glances at other parts of the body or room, if done naturally, provide a more effective way of relating and avoid the appearance of staring. It is important, however, to look into the eyes of a client a good share of the time. This provides a feeling of warmth and attention which increases the climate of trust so necessary to an effective counseling relationship.

2. Attentive body language: Communicating involves

much more than verbal behaviors. Some writers have indicated that as much as 80 to 85 percent of our communications may be nonverbal in nature. Our eyes, facial expressions, and body postures often speak much louder than our words in expressing how we really feel. You should be aware of how feelings are conveyed in this way. You will then present a true picture of how you are feeling and responding to the client. You will also be in a position to gain a more accurate understanding of the feelings which the client may be expressing in nonverbal ways.

The most attentive body posture is one where the counselor faces the client and is "open" in posture. A closed position (with arms and legs crossed, or facing partly away from client) is often interpreted by the client as boredom or disinterest on the counselor's part. A slight leaning forward, toward the client, on the other hand, is often helpful because it conveys warmth and involvement—a sense of presence and "being with" the client. Smiling is also seen as being warm and attentive.

Of course, all of these actions should be used in your own natural, most relaxed style. A rigid pattern of *only* sitting in one way or holding the arms in one position (for instance, *never* crossing them) will surely seem awkward, and will result in an uncomfortable feeling on the part of both you and your client.

To give yourself an idea of the importance of nonverbal cues in communication, try the following exercises:

Exercise 2: **Choose a partner and close your eyes. Spend two or three minutes in conversation with each other; then share your experiences. What nonverbal cues did** you miss the most by having your eyes closed?

Exercise 3: Next, spend two minutes in *silence* with your partner, just looking at each other. Examine the facial features, body build, clothing, etc., of this person. What do these things say about your partner? What kind of feelings did you experience looking at one another without talking? Why? Finally, close your eyes and try to describe your partner in detail. Let your partner do the same thing with you. Were you attentive enough to notice and remember minor details?

3. *Verbal following:* The third aspect of attending behavior is verbal following. Simply stated, this means concentrating on *what* the client is saying and how it is being said. Your role in verbal following is to avoid jumping to new topics. This can be done by concentrating on staying with the topic being discussed by the client or simply repeating key parts of what the client has said. This not only conveys that you have heard the client accurately but also encourages the client to continue without having to deal with irrelevant or premature topics introduced by you into his or her thinking process.

How the client is talking is often as important or more important than what he or she is saying. The client's tone of voice, spacing of pauses, choice of words, etc., may all serve to provide meaningful messages to an attentive observer and listener.

Attending behaviors provide an effective means for helping to establish rapport and trust in the early stages of the counseling relationship. The counselor who adopts and practices these will effectively help to move

44

the counseling process more quickly to a working stage. As a test, or for further practice in using these three attending skills in combination, try the following exercise:

Exercise 4: **Find two other persons and briefly explain the attending behaviors to them, or read them the preceding pages. Have one of your partners tell you about the "most wonderful day" in his or her life. You act as a helper by listening and practicing all of the active listening and attending skills. Don't try to say anything—just be attentive. The third person should observe and critique you on how you come across as a listener. Rotate roles if your partners want to try it too!**

EMPATHY, WARMTH, AND RESPECT

Empathy, warmth, and respect are best described as conditions to be achieved in the helping process. Because the counselor's use of these conditions indicates attentiveness and interest in the client, they are included here as part of effective listening. However, the practice of these conditions also may involve responding on the counselor's part and they just as easily could have been included in the following chapter. In either case, all three of these conditions are essential to the establishment of a caring, trusting relationship for counseling.

Empathy **is best described as a condition or state of being on the part of a counselor. It consists of three parts:**

1. Being able to "get inside" the other person's thinking or feelings; being able to understand the world *from his or her viewpoint* or frame of reference. Rogers

(*On Becoming a Person*, p. 284) describes this as the ability to "sense the client's world as if it were your own, but without ever losing the 'as if' quality."

2. The second part of empathy is placing the client's feelings into words which he or she can understand.

3. Finally, empathy involves being able to use these words to respond to clients in a way which will help them to know that you understand their experiences and feelings.

Empathy must be recognized as being different from *sympathy* which is usually not all that helpful. Empathy means "feeling with" the client whereas sympathy means feeling *sorry for* the client. This is an important distinction because most troubled persons are seeking understanding rather than sympathy.

Because accurate empathy is a difficult skill to develop, many persons fall into traps in trying to communicate in an empathetic or "feeling" way. Some of these traps as described by Egan (*Interpersonal Living*, pp. 124-127) include the following:

The cliché: responding with a superficial response, or using the phrases "I understand" or "I know what you mean" which have generally lost meaning through being overused.

Questioning: responding with a question **about** a feeling rather than responding with how you are experiencing the client's feeling.

Pretending to understand: responding as though you have understood the client's feelings when, in fact, you got lost in your own thoughts—or somewhere else.

Parroting: responding by restating exactly how the

client said he felt rather than how you experienced him or her as feeling.

Empathy can be demonstrated in either a low or a high form. Low empathy is communicating your understanding of the client's stated or superficial feelings. High empathy is understanding and communicating a deeper feeling than the client has actually expressed. Too much high level empathy in the earliest stages of the counseling relationship should be avoided because clients may come to believe that you have some magical power to "see inside" them. They may then stop revealing and exploring themselves to the extent needed for the counseling process to progress to a fruitful stage.

In summary, empathy is simply our ability to put ourselves in the place of other persons and see things through their frame of reference. It is *as though* we were those persons, yet we are maintaining our own separate identity and perspective as well. It does not mean that we *completely* understand the client. We probably could never fully understand another person because we are not exactly like any other in individual experience or makeup. Fortunately, such a complete understanding is not necessary. The fact that there are more similarities among persons than differences allows us to be helpful by trying to understand and because we know about or have had experiences or feelings which are *similar* to those being described by the client.

Warmth toward the client is ordinarily communicated nonverbally through the tone of voice, facial expressions, and gestures used by the counselor. Warmth is the creation of conditions which make the

47

client feel accepted and significant as a person. It is related both to empathy and respect as part of the "triangle of trust," or equal conditions needed for a trusting relationship to be created between the counselor and the client.

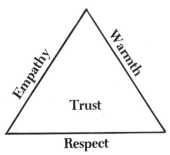

Warmth is that quality we tend to give naturally to those whom we understand and in whom we trust. We display warmth to these persons by smiling, speaking in soft tones, touching, and being close in proximity. The opposite characteristics of frowning, harsh speech tones, maintaining distance, and avoiding touch are usually viewed as cold or disinterested actions.

Respect is a quality which is closely related to warmth and acceptance. It means having faith in the client as a person of worth and potential. Respect is based on the value of a person in God's sight and not on just the behaviors that are current in that person's life. George Gazda (*Human Relations Development*, p. 78) defines respect as being open to involvement with the client. It is shown in the openness and genuineness of the counselor in relating to the client. Gerard Egan (*Interpersonal Living*, p. 148) describes respect as "being for" the client. He indicates that respect is shown by attending to the client, the counselor's regard of the client as a unique individual, and genuineness on the part of the counselor in dealing with the client. Egan (p. 151) summarizes the idea of respect by stating that "it is impossible to 'practice' respect in and by itself. Respect refers to a set of attitudes communicated to others and to behaviors embedded in the communication process."

Respect, as a part of acceptance, involves an element of expectancy. We are called to function in a role in which we not only accept people for what they are today but, more important, we accept them for what they are able to become tomorrow—and perhaps our help will be crucial to the dawning of that tomorrow!

Naturally, respect for a client implies that the counselor will not exploit the client for the counselor's own purposes. In this regard, for instance, disrespect for clients may be shown by counselors who attempt to impose their own beliefs or values on the clients they serve. This is a type of exploitation of which church leaders must be particularly aware. The role of spiritual leadership may make us eager to push a client to a re-membrance of the "true values" of life as professed and practiced in discipleship to God. However, the counselor role also dictates that clients must become aware of, and accept the influence of, these values for themselves before they will truly live by them. Thus, the counselor, rather than insisting on the client's acceptance of certain values, must instead provide opportunities for the client to explore and accept (or reaccept) these aspects of self. The uniqueness of the individual as a created being under God demands this respect.

Identifying Feelings

Identifying feelings can be described as "listening for meaning." It is a way in which the counselor seeks for the state of being behind the client's words; what the client is experiencing in terms of emotions rather than words. The identification and exploration of feelings is a vitally important part of the counseling process. The client must explore feelings before being able to identify or change any self aspects which may be influencing current attitudes or behaviors. Likewise, we as counselors cannot respond in a way to aid a client's exploration process unless we are able to identify or perceive the feelings being experienced by the client and use these in our subsequent interactions with the client.

There are three broad types or categories of feelings which a counselor should seek to identify. The first type is *surface feelings* which are fairly easy to recognize from the words used by the client, or from the obvious nonverbal signs displayed by the client through body postures, gestures, or facial expressions. Most of us can recognize a variety of emotions by nonverbal signs alone (see Exercise 6, p. 52).

The second type of feelings are *deeper feelings* which underlie the client's surface emotions. The counselor identifies this type of feeling by putting together various parts of the client's verbal and nonverbal behaviors. To do this, the counselor must ask, "What is this person saying verbally? What is this person saying non-verbally? What differences are there in these two ways of communicating or the feelings which appear to be expressed? If there is a difference, what does it mean? What feelings are being expressed by this client without the person's awareness?"

Finally, the counselor must look for *ambivalent* feelings or mixed emotions. These can also be noted by differences in verbal and nonverbal behaviors or by the manner in which the client speaks. For example, a client may experience grief at the loss of a near relative, but also feel and even display some relief if the relative had become an unusually heavy burden to care for before death.

Feelings can be *heard* in the client's words, *observed* in the client's body or face, or *felt* from the overall presence and demeanor of the client. The counselor can identify and reflect feelings through the use of a five-step process outlined by Gazda (*Human Relations Development*, pp. 57-58). These steps include the following:

- Identifying the client's general mood (positive or negative).
- Determining a specific kind of feeling.
- Determining the intensity of the feeling.
- Labeling or naming (in your own mind) the feeling with words similar to the client's usage of words.
- Responding with these words to the client and observing whether your feeling's identification was accurate and "hits the mark" with the client.

As feelings are identified, the counselor selectively attends to those which will be most helpful in the client's self exploration at that moment in the counseling process. The counselor must be careful, however, not to introduce his or her own feelings into what is "seen" in the client. This is one reason why it is so important for the counselor to maintain a full awareness of self feelings and reactions during the counseling session and separate these from the feelings which the client is experiencing. Of course, this does not imply that the counselor's feelings should always be hidden from the view of the client. To be a real person (authentic) to a client, the counselor should share personal feelings at appropriate points in the counseling process.

Identifying feelings is something we have learned to do almost unconsciously as we listen to others. Still, most of us are not nearly sensitive enough to be good counselors without additional training and practice in this essential skill. You are encouraged to try the following exercises to further practice feeling identification. However, if you are to be exceptionally sensitive to others' feelings and capable of accurately exposing these feelings to help clients explore their attitudes and needs you must constantly practice and sharpen your abilities in this essential skill.

Exercise 5: **Get several people to help you. Have participants tell about a recent or current problem which they may have experienced. As each participant tells about a problem, you try to respond to every *feeling* which you detect or observe in the speaker. You can respond to each suspected feeling by simply saying, "You feel *[name the emotion]*." If the person speaking denies this or seems confused, you missed! But keep trying. It takes time to learn new ways of relating effectively.**

Exercise 6: **Have a partner pantomime different emotions from the following list. Try to accurately identify emotions from the following list. Try to accurately** identify which emotion or feeling is being portrayed by your partner.

Feeling List

Grief	Disinterest	Fear	Hostility
Impatience	Anger	Resentment	
Puzzlement	Relaxation	Joy	
Anxiety	Confusion	Distrust	
Curiosity	Defensiveness	Reticence	

When you can identify 50 percent of these accurately, try having your partner make up some new ones to try on you.

CHAPTER 4

EFFECTIVE RESPONDING

INTRODUCTORY COMMENTS

The primary objective in the earliest stages of counseling is to permit the client's self exploration by establishing a climate of trust and acceptance, and by encouraging the client to talk in some detail about personal experiences. Achieving effective listening style is one way of accomplishing these objectives. As the client continues to pursue these self exploratory concerns, it soon becomes necessary for you, as a counselor, to interact with this person by responding in a way that will provide encouragement to continue talking. At the same time you must introduce meaningful information into the counseling sessions. Such response requirements demand that you learn to interact and respond (at least in the early stages) in a way which produces the least possible interjection of your own talk and ideas into the client's discussion.

Helpful responding can be accomplished through the use of "minimal encouragement responses." In addition, paraphrasing, reflection of client feelings, the use of certain types of questions, summarizing responses, focusing and structuring, and limited inter-pretations will help the client's self exploration process and further aid in moving the counseling relationship into an action or working stage. This chapter discusses these response categories, all of which are designed to be at least minimally facilitative (see Level Three below).

Carkhuff (*Helping and Human Relations*, Vol. 2, p. 315 ff.) has outlined a five-level model of responding which classifies responses in terms of their helpfulness to the client and whether the responses add to or detract from the verbal interchange between counselor and client. Level 1 responses are those verbal and behavioral expressions which *detract significantly* from the counseling process and the goals of counseling. Such responses fail to attend to the client, disregard client feelings, show a lack of respect for the client as an individual, or mask the counselor's genuine feelings concerning the encounter. Level 2 responses, by the counselor, *subtract noticeably* from the effect or expressions of the client, show a lack of respect in some ways, are somewhat less than genuine in terms of the counselor's true feelings. Such responses are somewhat harmful to the counseling process and do little to further meet the client's stated needs. Level 3 responses are at least *interchangeable* with those of the client. They are somewhat helpful at a minimally facilitative level because they express essentially the same meaning as the client's statements, communicate a "neutral" respect and concern for the client, indicate genuineness on the part of the counselor, and provide for some helpful self disclosure on the counselor's part.

Level 4 and 5 responses are the types of responses

ideally sought on the part of effective counselors. Level 4 responses *add noticeably* to the expressions of the client in terms of deeper feelings. They clearly communicate a deep respect and concern for the client and indicate a positive genuineness in counselor feelings and expressions. Level 5 responses are unusually effective and therapeutic communications. They *add significantly* to the feelings and meanings being expressed by a client (at a deeper level than expressed by client). They communicate the very deepest respect for the client as a person and provide an opportunity for the counselor to be freely and spontaneously "open" with the client to honestly approach discrepancies in the client's behavior in helpful ways. Level 4 and 5 responses are rarely totally a part of most persons' communication abilities and practice. However, the conscientious counselor will attempt to reach these levels in interacting with clients. Such responses demonstrate the counselor's complete willingness to be involved and are maximally effective in producing the most responsible counseling outcomes in terms of client change and/or coping capacity.

MINIMAL ENCOURAGEMENT RESPONSES

Allen Ivey, a noted human relations researcher and psychological educator, has identified a number of verbal responses which he has labeled "minimal encouragers to talk" (*Basic Attending Skills*, p. 21). These are short, neutral-type responses which counselors can use to convey interest and involvement to the client. They encourage the client to continue without really interrupting the flow of the client's thought processes.

Nonverbal encouragers include the attending behaviors outlined in chapter three plus head nodding, relaxed postures, and similar signs of interest or agreement. *Verbal* encouragement responses include simple phrases or single words which you can use to show that you are listening to and "with" the client. These include the use of words and phrases like "And then," "Uh-huh," "I see," or simply repeating the client's last words, or key words, to indicate that you are hearing and relating to the thoughts. Taken together with friendliness and nodding of the head, all of these brief verbal responses can go a surprisingly long way toward maintaining the client's exploration process with minimal interruptions from the counselor.

Silence, too, can often be used very effectively as a way of helping the client. If the counselor simply looks at or shows continued interest in the client at a pause in speech, the client may continue after a moment to collect his or her thoughts. Naturally, if the client fails to continue, the counselor may then wish to avoid an awkwardly long silence by saying something like, "Would you like to go on (or go into that a little further)?" The counselor should not be too quick to do this however. Often, such silences provide valuable "review" time and the client will proceed after a few seconds for internal review.

Try the following exercise for practice in using minimal encouragement responses:

Exercise 7: **Ask another person to help you by telling you all about his or her wedding day or a big date. Try to**

57

actively listen, using the attending behaviors *and* using minimal encouragement responses.

PARAPHRASING

Paraphrasing is another method of responding which allows the counselor to interact without introducing new discussion material which diverts the client away from focus on personal experience. Paraphrasing is the process of "feeding back" to the client a restatement (but in your own words) of what the client has expressed.

Example
Client: "It all seems so useless and depressing to me."
Counselor: "You're sad it happened and feel it wasn't really necessary."

Such a response provides an opportunity for the client to better understand his or her feelings by experiencing them in a different context while retaining the same specific feeling identification.

Paraphrasing is a more advanced form of attending behavior. Many beginning counselors make the mistake of overusing the paraphrase to the point where the client begins to feel that conversation is going in circles. The paraphrase is useful for helping the client stay in a specific frame of reference, but if overused by the counselor it can lead to frustration on the part of the client.

Exercise 8: **Ask someone to think over a real or imaginary problem that he or she would be willing to share with you. As the person tells you about this problem, try to use** your attending skills (eye contact, attentive body language, and verbal following) *plus* paraphrases as a way of continuing the conversation and enabling your partner to further explore feelings regarding this problem.

REFLECTING FEELINGS

Reflection of feeling is similar to paraphrasing except that the goal of the counselor is to avoid restating (in different words) what the client *said*. Here the counselor is, instead, responding only to the client's apparent *feeling* about what he or she is saying. The counselor's ability to reflect the feelings of the client is the client's proof that the counselor is interested in *understanding* rather than *evaluating* the client.

It perhaps goes without saying that most of us have been taught to (over)control our feelings. We have been told, "Act your age," and "Big boys don't cry," so often that we may have difficulty actually recognizing, experiencing, or evaluating some of our feelings. For this reason, it is important to be able to accurately reflect the feelings being experienced by another person if that person is to be helped to explore, evaluate, and accurately express his or her feelings—or to adapt them to produce less stressful modes of behavior. By "reflecting" client feelings accurately, you can keep the client's focus away from rationalizing (making excuses for) or intellectualizing (covering up with thinking about) his or her situation or attitudes.

In counseling, you may wish to consider the following aspects or points concerning the reflection of feeling:

- Shall I reflect only the superficial feeling of the client or a deeper feeling which he or she has not expressed but which I suspect exists?

- Will the selection of this particular feeling for reflection be meaningful for the client at this time?

- Should I add some additional meaning to this feeling as I reflect it?

- What words will be useful in reflecting this feeling back to the client?

You can answer these questions only if you have begun to develop an understanding of the person (client) with whom you are involevd (see empathy, chapter three). Furthermore, your understanding of the client must encompass and focus on the immediate here-and-now feelings of the client, since it is these feelings which, when admitted to awareness and explored, will tend to bear the most fruit in terms of client change.

Exercise 9: **Return to Exercise 5 in chapter three. Repeat it using a different partner (or the same partner with a different problem). This time, try to think through the four considerations listed before you make your "You feel _____" responses to your partner's feelings.**

QUESTIONING THE CLIENT

The best questions in counseling are those that are not asked! As long as a counselor is using repetitive questioning as a counseling technique, the client will continue to make statements *about* self rather than truly explore self.

Example
Counselor: "How long have you felt like this?"
Client: "Two months, I guess."
Counselor: "Do you feel low today, too?"
Client: "Yes."
Counselor: "Is your family still reacting the same way?"
Client: "Yes."

As is obvious, such a line of questioning could continue for some time without eliciting much information of value. Furthermore, such questions tend to create a situation in which the client becomes increasingly dependent upon the counselor by placing the responsibility for problem solving on the counselor's shoulders. After all, if you were being questioned for two or three counseling sessions, and providing answers to those questions, wouldn't you expect that at the end of the questioning the counselor would have some answers to your problems? Since pat solutions to problems are not usually forthcoming from the counselor, the client will simply resent the lengthy (and largely useless) questioning periods.

Questions also tend to reduce the client's self exploration because the counselor is the person placed "in charge" of deciding what will be talked about next and what data is desired. The client begins to assume that his or her role is simply to provide answers to whatever the counselor is asking—not to examine alternatives and make value choices which often require hard personal decisions. The counselor, on the other hand, will probably be making little use of the information anyhow, since it is usually difficult to be asking numerous questions and still remain an attentive listener. Thus, the most important overtones of the client's feelings and statements may be missed by the counselor.

Fortunately, most of these negative factors pertain primarily to *close-ended* questions. These are questions which are designed for the benefit of the counselor. They are to get information and usually require simple or short answers. Thus, they seldom produce much information about the client without the necessity of asking *more* questions (see preceding example).

Occasionally, close-ended questions have some useful purposes. They can provide needed personal data in a quick fashion. They can also be used by the counselor to move away from a topic or feeling which appears to be too much for the client to handle at that particular moment. As a rule of thumb, however, such a mode of questioning should be held to a minimum for the counseling to be most effective.

An alternative type of questioning, if used naturally rather than overused, can be quite helpful in encouraging a client to talk and provide helpful information at the client's own pace. This type of question is referred to as *open-ended*. It is designed to be a question which invites the client to "tell me about" some area being discussed. Such a question would normally begin with words such as "could," "would," or "how."

Example
"What made you decide that way?"
"How could you decide?"
"How has it been since last week when we talked?"

This type of question can help to begin an interview which picks up naturally where a previous interview ended. It can be used to get the client to further elaborate on some point or to focus the client's attention on a particular feeling. It provides a way to help clients move into areas of self where meanings and attitudes need to be clarified or values reexamined. Used in this manner, open-ended questioning is an effective counseling aid. The counselor must be careful not to use questioning to the exclusion of other more therapeutic forms of responding. Questioning, if overused, will quickly wear a client thin; listening will not!

SUMMARIZING

When people seek counseling help from you, they will be ready to talk, in most instances, about a variety of things which are weighing heavily on their minds. Often all the anxieties accumulated over many months will come bubbling forth as they attempt to include every possible detail of information or feeling which may be a factor in the problem they are experiencing. As you listen to the client spill out all of this information, you may feel overwhelmed by the details which will demand attention as the counseling progresses. It is likely that the client, too, will feel somewhat at loose ends over the sheer volume of material with which to deal.

It is useful at these points in counseling to respond in ways which summarize the client's talk and information in broader categories. This consolidation helps to focus the client's attention on the basic issues while leaving those of lesser importance to a later time—when they may appear less significant. In addition, summarizing statements, made by the counselor early in therapy, provide a climate in which the client can see that the counselor is getting the gist of what he or she is saying. This will suggest to the client that the counselor is understanding the client.

A summary response provides an opportunity for the counselor to convey understanding without having to remember or repeat verbatim *every*thing the client has just spoken. An example of the use of such a response follows.

Example

Client: "I'm not sure when all this began or even what caused it. Probably everything has something to do with it. I know my children and husband have contributed to how I feel, but then maybe it's just that we don't get along, any of us; except I do get along OK with people at work, when I'm not too nervous—which I always am at home I guess. I just think it's got a lot to do with a whole lot of things; home, the pressures on me with the kids and all, and I—I just don't know at all!"

Counselor: "It seems as if many things may have a bearing on it, but mostly you're feeling it's the people and your relationships at home that's at the core of it."

FOCUSING AND STRUCTURING

Summarizing is one method of focusing on a selected topic or group of topics revealed by a client. Another method is simply to give *selective attention* to certain words of the client while not responding to others at that particular time in the session. This type of focus structures the interview to provide an opportunity for the client to narrow his or her own focus to a few topics capable of being handled during that period of counseling time.

The exact focus chosen by you, the counselor, will, of course, depend greatly on what has gone on before, what appears natural to deal with in that particular session, and how you feel the client will relate to and explore a given topic. Thus, from all the content of even a single verbalization, the counselor must choose to respond in one of many possible ways.

Example

Client: "I'm so nervous about this fall and starting college. I won't have anyone I know going to State University and I'm afraid my shyness will keep me from making new friends very quickly. Sometimes, I think I'd just be happier staying at home and getting a job or something."

As a counselor, you could focus on any number of points in responding to the content of what the client has said. You may wish to focus on

A. the client's nervousness.
B. getting started at college.
C. aloneness.
D. the client's tendency to be shy.
E. difficulties in making new friends.
F. advantages/disadvantages of staying at home.
G. work vs. college attendance as goals.

Your responses, then, would vary depending on how you wished to structure or focus the session at that moment:

A. "You're feeling pretty scared at how fast fall is coming up on you."
B. "There's a lot involved in getting started at a new place—especially college."
C. "Not knowing anyone at college will be pretty lonely for you at first."
D. "You may be alone quite a while because of your shyness about making new friends."
E. "Making new friends isn't easy and you're afraid that, for you, it will be more difficult than for most people."
F. "It's difficult to let go of the homelife you've been accustomed to all these years."
G. "Sometimes just getting a job around here seems like an easier route than going off to college and kind of starting over."

Obviously, the way in which counselors structure their responses will greatly affect what clients will talk about or deal with next in counseling. Thus, while you will attempt to avoid interjecting content not raised by the client, you can and should make responses which responsibly direct the client toward one or more of the topics which the client has introduced into the discussion. If you fail to do this, you will find yourself spending many counseling sessions discussing the same topics over and over without moving deeper than the superficial level or ever satisfactorily resolving the issues raised. Thus, focusing and structuring provide a method for you to become more active as a person while preserving the client's agency to introduce and work with the topics which most concern him or her. Used responsibly (and shall I say intuitively) by an effective counselor, focusing and structuring responses will help the client to focus on specific problem-solving behaviors earlier in counseling than would otherwise be the case.

As a way of helping you learn to focus on selected topics and structure conversation toward effective ends, try the following exercise:

Exercise 10: **Once again, obtain the assistance of your faithful friend! Have him or her relate an event which he or she considers to be "one of the scariest times in my life." As you respond, try to focus on different types of subjects, feelings, etc., introduced by your partner. Observe the directions which the conversation takes after each of your responses. Naturally, you will have to wait your turn to speak before responding.**

INTERPRETING

Interpretation is the skill of providing a new perspective or point of view to something, or "renaming" it. It is an essential skill to develop if a counselor hopes to be able to understand clients at more than a superficial level or lead clients to explore facets of self not yet recognized by the clients themselves. Interpretation is an act of creativity on the part of the counselor. It is a "leap beyond" what was said to pick up something which was *inferred* or may be "behind" the feelings or statements of the client. Thus, it is a potentially more powerful response than simply re-stating or paraphrasing because it opens up areas of exploration with which the client may not yet be able to deal. It brings an "insight" to the client (if he or she is ready to deal with the topic) which was not previously a matter of consciousness—at least not in terms of being openly admitted to the counselor.

Because of the effects of interpretation, you must be particularly sensitive to the timing of such responses and to the readiness of the client to deal with the material introduced. When the client immediately follows an interpretation with a denial, confusion, or change of subject, you can be relatively assured that the client is not yet ready to deal with the possibilities suggested by the interpretation. Of course, there is the possibility, too, that you managed to infer something which was not correct! In such an event, the client has every right to be confused.

To clarify the concept of interpreting as opposed to restating or paraphrasing what the client has actually said, note the following example.

Example

Client: "I just don't know about him. He is nice one minute and then can be mean the next."

Counselor (restating): "He's mean then."

Counselor (paraphrasing): "He seems pretty inconsistent to you."

Counselor (interpreting): "He's so inconsistent, you've just about given up on him."

Notice that, in interpretation, the counselor has made the leap beyond what the client actually said. The counselor is *assuming* the client is about ready to give up on the person being referred to in the conversation. If the counselor's guess is correct, the client may be able to partially or wholly admit this possibility and begin to deal with the alternatives available. If the counselor is wrong, the client will deny the possibility by saying something like "Oh, no! Nothing like that" or "Why would I do that?" Obviously, if wrong, the counselor will have momentarily introduced some confusion into the discussion and set back the development of the trusting and understanding aspects of the relationship—at least temporarily. Thus it is important that you be judicious in your use of interpretation, making interpretations as *tentative* possibilities based on all that the client has said or felt up to this point in the counseling encounter. If the client denies the interpretation, but you still feel strongly that it is a possibility, you should return to it later for a second trial rather than pushing the issue with the client. It is possible that at a later point in counseling the client will be able to recognize the validity of the interpretation given in a new context.

As ways of testing your creativity and ability to interpret, try the following exercises:

Exercise 11: **If someone gave you a thousand empty tin cans, what are all the uses which you could make of them?**

Exercise 12: **Select ten people at random from those you know. Consider one prominent feature or characteristic of each's personality. How do you think that feature or personal characteristic developed? What alternative ways might it have developed? (Use your imagination!)**

Exercise 13: **Ask your family members to tell you about their dreams for the next few days. As they tell you about the dreams, try to make interpretations (to yourself) by drawing together several aspects of the dream on the basis of what you know about that family member. Are**

there any alternative interpretations possible (too much pizza the night before!)?

Interpreting is a skill which can be only partially learned by reading about it. The full development of your potential to make accurate and *helpful* interpretations can be derived only from practice while counseling or talking with others. Naturally, playing at "psychologist" with all your friends at inappropriate times will do little to win you friends or help you influence people. Save your interpretations for times when you feel reasonably assured that you have picked up on something which not only exists at a deeper level in the client but will also be helpful to that person if brought to light for consideration *at this time*. Don't try to put your world on the client by giving your favorite interpretations of the events brought out in the client's life. Such interpretations will almost always be inaccurate and harmful to clients' attempts to explore their own frame of reference and self system beliefs. Interpreting is one of the truly artful parts of the counseling process; use it with the taste of an artist!

CHAPTER 5

EFFECTIVE INFLUENCING

INTRODUCTORY COMMENTS

Many professional counselors believe that counselor influence has no place in the counseling relationship. They claim that client self exploration will surely be hampered if counselors let their own values or attitudes enter into the counseling process, or attempt to suggest or persuade in any manner. Such beliefs, however, seem contradictory to the hypothesis that a client seeks out a counselor specifically because the client desires the assistance of someone whom he or she believes will be influential in helping to solve the problems with which the client is confronted. Such beliefs are also in opposition to our knowledge of healing practices which have, for centuries, made use of persuasion and suggestion in helping persons achieve emotional health or readjustment. Both ancient shamans and current tribal witch doctors have made heavy and effective use of such methods to effect "cures" in their patients. Current psychotherapist practitioners also make use of suggestion, either deliberately or unconsciously, to encourage hope in their clients.

Certainly, there is little real doubt but that any counselor will exert some influence in the counseling sessions. Counselors who are being themselves—genuinely authentic and real—in interacting with the client can hardly avoid (nor should they) revealing some personal attitudes and values relative to the topics under discussion. Likewise, the client will undoubtedly weigh the counselor's responses, opinions, and actions carefully if a reasonable level of respect and trust has been developed between the two persons. Thus, influencing exists for better or for worse in counseling. The real concern is whether such influencing *enhances* the client's progress toward responsible individuality or *retards* such progress. A counselor who attempts to persuade or "hard sell" the client to a system of values or a course of action which the counselor advocates may prove to be an obstacle in the client's long-term growth as a person. Thus, influencing, to be used effectively, must be used with wisdom.

THE ROLE OF SELF DISCLOSURE

Close personal relationships develop as a result of self disclosure on the part of the individuals involved. The level or degree of intimacy is related to the amount and depth of self disclosure. Conversely, the amount of self disclosure can serve as an index of how much trust and mutual respect exist between two persons. Thus, an effective marriage—as an example—can be partially measured by the intimacy and depth of the partners' self disclosures to one another. Such self disclosures will help to establish the trust and mutual respect needed to produce both individuality and complementary aspects in the marriage.

Joseph Luft and Harry Ingram (*Group Processes*, p. 11) designed a graphic model to show how various communicative aspects of self, related to self disclosure, change as a relationship grows. This model is referred to as the "Johari Window" after its originators. The "window" shows an area of self known to others but "blind" to the self; an area of "hidden" self which is known to the self but is not revealed to most others; and, last, an area that is not known by either the self or others (an unconscious area). The model can be depicted as follows:

	Known to Self	Unknown to Self
Known to others	#1 Free to Self Others	#2 Blind to Self; seen by others
Unknown to others	#3 Area hidden from others	#4 Unknown Self

At the beginning of a relationship, the model might look like this, according to its originators:

1	2
3	4

Because little interaction has taken place, the lack of trust or exploration possibilities has acted to leave the blind, hidden, and unknown areas relatively large. Communication between persons in this type of relationship would tend to remain at a superficial or casual level. Because little trust has been established, there would be very little opportunity for each person to gain greater insights into the other's own way of acting and reacting. Topics of conversation would remain in "safe" areas and the parties would tend to avoid discussing any personal issues in any depth. Thus, clarification or exploration of personal issues would be hampered.

As a relationship develops, however, the model might look more like this:

1	2
3	4

In this type of relationship and communication pattern, in-depth issues are fully explored. The trust that is present between the two persons is both mutual and operational at a high level. The parties are able to learn and grow in a mutually supportive relationship where more personal thoughts and feelings become open for "free" discussion and consideration. Defensive attitudes are dropped and risk taking behavior is increased.

Self disclosure with a significant other person can

provide a means for examining self (particularly the spiritual self). It can lead a client into taking responsible actions to restructure his or her life and deal more effectively with the trials of daily existence which result from our environment and our reactions to it. Some writers have indicated that our emotional health may even depend on confronting (revealing) and examining our irresponsibility and often self*ish* attitudes and ways of living. Self disclosure is also viewed by others as a request for support and social acceptance. People who are poor self disclosers tend to encounter loneliness because no one can really know them as persons. People tend to like and gravitate toward persons who are open in their relationships and communications.

In spite of the importance of self disclosure as a part of establishing and maintaining effective interpersonal relationships, many persons in our society experience great difficulty in openly expressing their emotions. This seems to be particularly true if such feelings are negative (e.g., expressing anger toward another person). Because self disclosure skills are difficult to learn to use appropriately, many persons shy away from openly expressing their reactions to the present or relating past experiences which affect their reactions to the present. Because of just such tendencies, the counselor must frequently serve as a model in the appropriate use of skills such as self disclosure.

Self disclosure statements by the counselor are for the client's benefit. To be effective, such statements must relate to or parallel what the client has said or experienced. Self disclosure is not used as a means of building up one's own importance or revealing one's experience simply to gain attention. The counselor should avoid the "You think that's bad, listen to what happened to me" type of self disclosure.

The counselor's own self disclosure should provide a beneficial experience for the client. This occurs when such statements are related to the counselor's present feelings rather than past feelings, and when the statements are direct reports rather than disguised reports of the counselor's true feelings. *Feelings* are emphasized rather than thoughts. Furthermore, the counselor must strive to be self relating as well as self disclosing. One can—and often does—self disclose without being very self involved. Self disclosure should serve as a way of sharing one's self with another.

Unfortunately, many beginning counselors (and a few persons who play at being "psychology-oriented") tend to adopt an almost worshipful attitude toward openness and make self disclosure a rite to be performed anywhere or any time. This is clearly inappropriate. Telling your life story in intimate detail to a casual acquaintance on a bus bound for Tallahassee does little to improve your total effectiveness as a person! Furthermore, since the relationship is not meant to be continued, such embarrassing revealments are simply a burden and a nuisance to the listener.

Neither is self disclosure by a counselor in counseling an end unto itself. Appropriate timing and purposes of self disclosing statements must be borne in mind by the counselor. Gerard Egan (*Interpersonal Living*, pp. 47-53) has outlined some working criteria which are useful in this regard. You can use these criteria (see the following paragraph) to determine when and how to appropriately use the skill of self disclosure during counseling.

Self disclosures by the counselor are most helpful to the client when the self disclosure

- is directed toward a goal of the counseling session(s).
- is limited to an amount and intimacy level appropriate to the goal or purpose for which the statement was made.
- will improve the overall quality of the relationship.
- is timely (i.e., emerges from what is currently being discussed in the session).
- is placed in a present tense and a reason for it is provided. (Example: "I feel_____right now, because I once had a similar thing happen to me. I . . ."
- involves a reasonable risk; you are willing to trust the client with any personal information revealed.
- is given in a shared context—to help with the problem you are both working on.

Counselors use the working criteria outlined to reveal detailed information about themselves which is in keeping with the client's expressed interests or needs and the goals of counseling. Counselors attempt to keep themselves fully open to clients, including any negative feelings which they may have. They maintain personal privacy about matters unrelated to the counseling while employing self disclosure in a way which constructively enhances the client's open-ended inquiry into self.

As there are appropriate times and methods of self disclosing, there are also many blocks to self disclosure—both by the client and the counselor. These should be recognized by the counselor and circumvented where appropriate. Our culture tends to foster "hiding" attitudes to accomplish actions or to make personal gains. Often our family relationships are such that being open about feelings and experiences is not encouraged. Sometimes we hide in our shells because we fear a careful examination of our self structure system. We fear rejection by others if they know about certain aspects of us or about causes of some of our feelings of guilt or shame. Or we may not wish to face the responsibility of owning up to our true value systems or certain ways we view ourselves as being.

The counselor must overcome some of these fears and model communication methods which enhance the client's opportunities to grow through purposeful self examination. Self disclosures, genuinely and trustingly made, appropriately timed, and related to the goals of counseling, contribute to client growth. Self disclosures made by the counselor to satisfy his or her own needs do not enhance the counseling process for the client.

Exercise 14: **Try drawing what your personal Johari Window might look like for each of the following relationships. Your relationship and communications with**

Your father
Your mother
A brother or sister
Your spouse
A casual acquaintance at work
God

Are there differences in what or how much you communicate to each of these persons? To God? If so, why do you think this is true?

Exercise 15: Draw a Johari Window with four equal areas. List in each quarter the topics of conversation that might be included in your free, blind, hidden, unconscious areas. Consider introducing more of these topics into your conversations with a close personal friend.

Exercise 16: Sit down with a friend and share your answers to the following incomplete sentences:
   I am most helpless when . . .
   I am happiest when . . .
   I feel guilty about . . .
   I last prayed about . . .
   My most important value is . . .
   Right now I am most concerned about . . .
   My spiritual self status can best be described as . . .

Try to think of more things about yourself which you feel would be helpful to share with this other person.

Exercise 17: Choose one casual acquaintance or work colleague with whom you normally speak daily. Do not inform him or her of what you are doing. For the next week, try to be as open as you feel comfortable in being with this person. Deliberately, but unobtrusively, try to interject *timely* and *related* personal feelings and experiences into your conversations with this person. At the end of one week, assess the impact this experiment has had on your conversations and relationship with this other person.

EXPRESSION OF FEELINGS AND EMOTIONS

Closely related to self disclosure is the need for counselors to learn appropriate expression of their own feelings and emotions. A counselor's willingness to deal with personal feelings openly in the counseling relationship encourages the client to do the same. There are, however, effective and ineffective ways to express personal feelings. The counselor needs to be familiar with and actively use effective emotional expression methods in the process of counseling.

Many counselors fear that if emotions (particularly their own) are allowed to enter into the counseling interaction the uniqueness and productivity of the relationship will be lost. This fear is especially strong when negative emotions (anger, resentment, etc.) are being felt by the counselor. Yet the counseling process does not suffer because emotions are present (it would be dull indeed if they weren't) but rather because emotions are not well used.

As a counselor you must learn to avoid the role of emotional sterility in your relationship with clients. As the process of counseling and self systems interactions unfolds you cannot avoid experiencing many feelings about both yourself and the other person. The degree of effectiveness and responsibility with which you express such feelings will—in large measure—account for how useful the counseling interaction will prove to be for the client. Fortunately, there are a number of principles to guide you in effectively monitoring and expressing your feelings during counseling.

One such principle in dealing with and expressing your own emotions is not to deny them. Emotions are a part of total self awareness and are legitimate in that they *are* there—at least in one's awareness. If you attempt to repress them or deny their existence, you simply gloss over a part of the meaning of that moment in your life and in your interaction with this other person. For this reason, it is important to recognize and be aware of your emotions, although you may responsibly *choose* to delay or control the expression of a particular emotion.

It is important, however, to deal with emotions relatively soon after you become aware of them. This is a second principle concerning expression of feeling. Saving up your feelings like green stamps usually results in an overreaction when you finally do decide to cash them all in on someone. The key to emotional expression is control, not repression.

A third principle of emotional expression by the counselor is that feelings should be relayed to the client gradually—particularly if such feelings are quite negative in tone. Constructive expression does not imply that the counselor has any positional right to use personal feelings as a license either to attack or manipulate the client. Neither does it imply that the counselor must be brutally honest! If personal feelings are introduced in an honest but humane way, they will be accepted by the client—if the relationship has been appropriately developed.

Expression of personal feelings and emotions can theoretically be handled in one of three possible ways:

- *Passively:* disguising your feelings so that they are conveyed in a weak manner to the client, or keeping your feelings inside and expressing very little to the client about how you are experiencing your relationship.

- *Aggressively:* dumping out all your feelings (positive and negative) in a manner which either overwhelms the client or places her/him on the defensive.

- *Assertively:* firmly and calmly expressing your emotions in a manner which deals with the issue or feeling involved but leaves the door open to further communicate with the client.

Obviously, assertive expression is most helpful to you and the client. You come across as a responsible person, capable and willing to express yourself openly and assert your right to be heard. Yet the client need not be defensive (if confronted with a negative feeling) or overwhelmed (if confronted with an overly positive feeling). A model of effective communication and interpersonal interaction is set forth for the client to use as a guide in his or her own expressions of feeling as well as in social relationships outside the counseling session. Finally, the door is left open for discussion which allows the two of you to grow in your understanding of each other and yourselves.

Exercise 18: Try to remember or picture yourself in some past situation where you have experienced each of the following feelings. First, try to express all of the feelings and emotions connected with the situation or scene, as you remember them, in another single word which means the same thing as the word given. Next, go over each scene again and try to express all of your related feelings in a short sentence. Finally, try to describe all of the feelings connected with each scene in terms of what you felt like *doing* at that time.

Example: "afraid"
(imagine a past situation)
1. "Scared"
2. "I felt shaky all over."
3. "I wanted to run away but my legs were weak."

Try it with each of the following emotions:

Fear	Trust	Excitement
Joy	Smugness	Reflection
Sorrow	Pride	Calmness
Satisfaction	Happiness	Nervousness

CONCRETENESS

Often clients are not accustomed to dealing with their feelings in a direct or specific way. As a result, they may make vague or generalized statements or be unable to identify specific feelings, behaviors, or concerns. To alleviate such tendencies, the counselor must learn to be specific or concrete in communicating with the client. As the counselor makes use of detailed, concise responding, the client learns to be direct and concise in describing specific values, feelings, and events. Concreteness in communicating with clients also insures that the counselor's responses remain emotionally close or "tuned in" to the client's own statements of feeling. This encourages accuracy in understanding the client, the events surrounding the client's situation, and the client's way of responding to such events. It also directly influences the client to deal with specific concerns and problem areas. This is es-

83

sential if the client is to later engage in effective problem solving.

Concreteness, or being specific, is modeled by the counselor in two ways: through the counselor's use of direct, specific, and detailed statements in responding to the client and by being specific in relating her or his own statements and experiences to the client.

Example

Client: "I don't understand people sometimes."

Counselor: "I feel that because you don't develop friendships easily, people tend to avoid you and you do not have the opportunity to really get to know them."

Client: "I sometimes find things boring."

Counselor: "Could this boredom be stemming from the fact that you and your husband don't talk to one another anymore?"

Practicing this kind of specificity and clarity in communication aids the client in identifying the exact conflict or problem areas involved. It also helps to avoid the "distance" that develops between persons who speak in generalities or use vague statements to communicate.

Your use of concreteness should vary during the counseling process depending on the stage of the counseling you are currently engaged in. In the earliest stages, concreteness is stressed in an effort to help keep the client close to the specific concerns involved and to aid the counselor in identifying and understanding the exact nature of those concerns. In the middle stages of counseling, concreteness is used somewhat less since exploration by the client may specifically require a freer exploration of how the identified problems relate to other broader aspects of the client's life. During the final stages of counseling, the use of concreteness again comes into play as the client must choose between specific action alternatives in search of solutions to the identified problems.

Try the following exercise in using concreteness with another person:

Exercise 19: **Select several recent experiences which you have had. Try to tell another person about these experiences, first by using vague terms and then by specifically stating the feelings and behaviors which accompanied these experiences. Ask your partner to tell about some experiences also and try to reflect statements and feelings by using responses which specifically identify your understanding of your partner's feelings and behaviors in the situation being related to you.**

GENUINENESS

Genuineness on the part of the counselor means being free from playing a role or hiding behind a facade, being who one really is. Counselors who are genuine in relationships with clients will be willing to reveal honest motivations for saying or doing what they do. They will be willing to show their inner life in a nondefensive, open way and will reveal themselves in constructive ways to clients. They will be able and willing to commit themselves to another person in a relationship of psychological closeness where the hidden self aspects are kept to a minimum. The counselor will be what C. H. Patterson (*Relationship Counseling and Psycho-*

therapy, p. 62) has referred to as "a real person in a real encounter."

In reflecting genuineness, the counselor will make statements which are in keeping with real, personal feelings. However, genuineness does not imply that the counselor has total freedom of expression. Genuineness must be tempered with a concern for the client's ability to handle various kinds of feelings. Obviously, the counselor's role is not to add to the client's low self esteem by relating feelings which are brutally honest. Rather, any negative feelings or opinions which contradict the client's position must be revealed in a gradual or constructive way. Genuineness can be for good or bad; a counselor who is rigid, exploitive, or hostile would not, of course, be therapeutic by being her or his real self. It is doubtful, though, that such a counselor would be helpful in any case.

The easiest way to identify appropriate genuineness on the part of the counselor is to measure it in terms of authentic involvement with the client. The genuine counselor does not play a role as a therapist. Rather, such a counselor *is* therapeutic, using genuineness in a way which is helpful to the client rather than harmful.

IMMEDIACY

Immediacy refers to the "here-and-now" or current interaction between client and counselor. It also refers to the communication between these persons about their current relationship. The essence of immediacy is *presence* and *mutuality* in the immediate moment. Immediacy is concerned with the give and take of the relationship in which client and counselor are engaged.

It is the purposeful act of talking about the interpersonal encounter. Thus, at the lowest levels of immediacy the counselor would ignore the client's actions and words if these related to the relationship or the counselor. At higher levels of immediacy, the counselor would directly express and deal with the client's words and actions which appeared to be directly related to the relations between the two persons.

The counseling relationship serves as a "microscope" through which the counselor can identify the client's behaviors in ordinary relationships outside of counseling. For this reason, immediacy is of considerable importance because it reflects the client's understanding of a relationship and/or responses to other persons under similar circumstances. Because immediacy serves as a reflector on the relationship, it is particularly useful for the counselor to focus on the immediate relationship during periods when the counseling process seems stalled or at a plateau in terms of progress. It is also important as a skill which is prerequisite to the joint cooperation of counselor and client in problem-solving and goal-setting stages of counseling.

Egan (*Interpersonal Living*, p. 202) describes immediacy as a complex skill which involves a mixture of empathy, self disclosure, and confrontation. It requires the counselor to perceive what is happening in the counseling relationship, to be able to skillfully communicate that perception at the appropriate time, and, finally, to have the courage to communicate the perception.

Immediacy is a transition skill. It is used more sparingly at first because its effectiveness depends on

87

the client and counselor's establishment of trust in the respect for one another. In the middle stages of counseling, tentative uses of immediacy are helpful to move the process forward and to gently confront the client with his/her modes of interacting with another person—especially when such actions or words of the client tend to relate to the problem situation which is in focus for the client at that particular time in the session. At later stages, open communication and self disclosure practices on the part of both persons frequently make the concentration on immediacy of less importance, since its use has then become more natural. The client and counselor will have evolved toward a relationship which is constantly "immediate" in that there is no reluctance on the part of either party to explore any facet of their interaction, particularly if the client can apparently benefit from such interpersonal communication.

Exercise 20: **Ask a friend to sit down with you while a third person acts as an observer. Engage your friend in a five or ten minute conversation about your goals as a counselor, how you see your skills as being developed, etc. After the two of you have talked for the stated time period, the third person (observer) will relate how he or she viewed the two of you in terms of feelings and thoughts which you may have had but didn't raise in the conversation with each other. Were there any immediate issues between you that were not raised in the con- versation itself? Explore these with one another.**

FEEDBACK

Feedback is a task skill that is related to both self

disclosure and confrontation. Its purpose is to provide information to clients about their behavior and how it affects you, the counselor. Such feedback information, of course, must be placed in a constructive context since a client will likely become defensive if such a context is not used. This defensiveness, if aroused, will hinder the client's reception and utilization of the information you are attempting to provide.

Your feedback should focus on the client's behaviors *as observed by you*. What you *infer* as possible client thoughts or actions is not as effective—if used as feedback—as those things which you have actually observed. You should use descriptions of what occurred rather than your judgment of whether a certain behavior was right or wrong. Furthermore, either/or situations should be avoided if possible; that is, your feedback should be cast in "more or less" terms. Feedback should be focused on behaviors related to a *specific* situation—preferably the here and now of the session itself; the sharing of ideas rather than an "I'll give advice—you listen" approach.

Focusing on giving feedback is more helpful if it allows for the exploration of alternatives and is given in the amount which the client can utilize at that time. It should be focused on what has been said rather than explanations of *why* it was said. Finally, it is used as a mode of sharing perspectives on client behaviors or words.

Example (client tends to overtalk, interrupt, and listens only superficially to what other persons are saying)
Counselor: "You say people tend to avoid you lately? You haven't . . ."

Client: "Yes, I don't know why" (interrupting).

Counselor: "How do you act in talking with others; what do you do that might 'turn people off'?"

Client: "Well, I just listen and try not to interrupt or anything, I guess."

Counselor: "Did you realize that you just interrupted me? Was that just excitement or what?"

Client: "Oh! I guess I did. Maybe I do that more than I realize."

Counselor: "It's a common problem, but we could work on it if you like."

In this example, the counselor is able to provide feedback on behaviors of the client in the immediate time frame, with the assumption that such behaviors may also affect the client's relationships outside of counseling. The counselor draws attention to an annoying habit of the client, yet allows an "escape" mechanism with the use of the phrase, "Was that just excitement or what?" This provides the client an opportunity to consider a possibility without being accused of being like that at all times.

Feedback is a way of returning your feelings and experiences connected with the client's behaviors and words as used in the counseling session itself. It is not a method of attacking the client; rather it is a way of intimately sharing yourself with the client so as to allow the client an opportunity for better understanding and exploration of self. In this sense, it is a valuable task skill and one which is prerequisite to both the establishment of an effective counseling climate and progress in later problem-solving stages of counseling.

CONSTRUCTIVE CONFRONTATION

Learning how to provide feedback and mastering use of the skill of immediacy are essential elements in the use of constructive confrontation. Confrontation is the skill of aiding clients to become aware of discrepancies. These discrepancies may involve differences between what clients are feeling and saying; what they are thinking and doing; what they are and what they would like to be; or what they really are compared to what they experience themselves as being. Confrontation is an invitation to clients to examine personal discrepancies in feelings or behaviors and to move beyond insight to action in changing unproductive behaviors.

The possibility of the counselor abusing the skill of confrontation is strong. Confrontation is often misused as is witnessed by the methods of some popular group movements in the recent past. Confronting another person requires *skill* and *caring*. Confrontation is not designed to be punitive by nature; neither is it delivered in the form of an accusation against the client or demand to change. Judgments, sarcasm, and criticism have no place in constructive confrontation. Rather, a productive confrontation will be a *description* of counterproductive behaviors and their probable impact on the client. Confrontation is used to provide the client an opportunity to evaluate self from a new perspective.

It is important that the skill of confronting not be used as a substitute for, or as an alternative to, understanding. The right to confront another person must be *earned*. The counselor should have a commitment to involvement in the counseling process. The counselor must have learned to be self disclosing, and to be aware of self in order to know "where she/he is coming from" in terms of the confrontation. Counselors strive to accurately understand other persons at the deepest levels and are also willing to be personally confronted without being defensive. Effective confronting always involves a high level of empathy toward, and respect for, the client.

There are a number of possible ways a confrontive statement can be presented, and in the earlier stages of counseling confrontation should be used only in a relatively tentative manner. The intensity or degree of confrontation can be decreased or made easier for the client to accept by preceding the confrontation with a positive statement, couching the confrontation in general terms (e.g., "some people feel that. . ."), using humor to make the confrontation less "heavy," or including an escape for the client within the confrontation itself (e.g., "perhaps I'm just imagining this but it seems that I hear you saying_____ but see you doing _____. Have I misunderstood what you were telling me?"). Confrontations are often easier for the client to accept if the counselor builds on the client's recognized strengths (e.g., "John, you seem to be very good at making effective choices. This causes me to wonder why in this case. . ."). Finally, confrontations should be presented gradually, keeping in mind the mental, physical, or emotional state of the person being confronted.

Confronting a client with challenges to make changes calls for delicate work on the part of a counselor. The counselor invites a client to examine some discrepancy in behavior only when it will help the client gain perspective rather than require the client to defend that behavior. The best confrontations are those which challenge a client to use personal strengths and encourages (calls) them to responsible action.

Examples

Client: "I think I'll have to give up my Sunday school class. I've tried hard, but everything seems disorganized and I don't think the kids are learning anything from me at all. We're simply not getting anywhere."

Counselor: "It all seems useless to you right now. Everything seems unplanned and yet I am wondering how this could happen with your past experience as a schoolteacher. Have you established any goals or objectives for each class?"

Client: "I'm trying really hard to work it all out with Martha, but I just haven't got the patience to deal with everything much longer."

Counselor: "It's tough to keep going sometimes. You say you haven't enough patience. I don't know . . . it seems as though you've been extraordinarily patient up to now, which is evidence of your ability to be patient. Is it just that you're ready to give up and don't *want* to be patient anymore?"

Exercise 21: Think about each member of your immediate family (or work group). What does he or she do that contributes best to the family or work setting? Write down several of these good qualities or strengths for each person. Over the next week, attempt to find an appropriate time to use these strengths in conjunction with *gently* confronting the family member about a weakness which you perceive that person to have. You may wish to concentrate on only one individual at a time (each week).

Example
Son Johnny is quite adept at woodworking and creating things but hates to carry trash out to curb and often "forgets." You would like to confront him with his lack of responsibility in carrying out his assigned chores, but want to avoid a running argument. Later in week: "Son, I've been thinking about how good you seem to be at building things. It occurred to me that the trash would be easier to get out on time if we bought some material and you built some sort of cart for the cans. What do you think—could you build something like that?"

PROBLEM SOLVING AND CONFLICT MANAGEMENT

Facilitative listening, responding, and influencing skills are essential to the development and progress of an effective counseling relationship. However, all of these skills are simply preparatory to the engagement of the client and counselor in the tasks of resolving problems and taking steps to manage the client's conflicts with other persons. The facilitative relationship, so carefully built and maintained by the counselor, now serves as a foundation for the difficult work of making decisions, resolving problems, and setting responsible behavior goals which will alleviate or reduce the client's emotional conflicts or stressful environmental circumstances.

Problem solving and conflict management involve the task of leading the client through an exploration of the following:

94

- What are the events leading up to the problem or conflict?
- How does the client view this problem?
- How do others in the client's life view this problem?
- How does the problem *involve* the client?
- What is the client's contribution to the problem?
- What must the client *do* to change the circumstances? What is he or she *willing* to do?
- Is there a mutually acceptable solution? If not, what are the reasonable alternatives?
- What acceptable ways are there for taking steps to solve the problem?
- What decisions must be made and what goals must be accomplished to assure progress in solving the problem?

These exploratory processes actually take place throughout the counseling sessions. The events leading up to the problem or conflict and how the client views the problem are usually brought out with fair clarity during the first few counseling sessions (although deeper problems may be disclosed later). How *others* view the problem may be assessed either through what the client says or, preferably, by their involvement in the counseling itself.

The next three exploratory tasks are the most difficult and often require the longest part of the total time spent in counseling the client. Clients' recognition of the full extent of their own involvement in this problem, how they feel and react to it, and what their contributions to it are constitute difficult tasks. It is in the conduct and accomplishment of these tasks that client self awareness and self acceptance become of critical importance. Most often, clients resist the responsibility and knowledge that they have contributed to the circumstances in which they find themselves or the disturbed feelings which they hold. Frequently, they are only vaguely aware of the true feelings which they may have toward the problem and/or toward others who are involved in it. Such feelings can often be explored through having a client reverse roles and assume the role of the other person(s) involved.

The next step is also one that takes considerable time to accomplish. Most emotional problems are perceptual in nature and clients typically perceive themselves as the "victims" of someone or something else. They often believe that all of their emotional chaos would be cleared up immediately *if only* "they" or "he" or "she" would do such and such. What the *client* must do to change his or her unfortunate circumstances is—more often than not—difficult for the client to accept. Yet one rarely has the power to force others to make major changes or to alter an environment without making substantial changes in one's own accepted routines. We can accept or change only ourselves or our own reactions to outside events. This is why accepting self responsibility will always remain a vital prerequisite to more effective and satisfactory modes of living.

Most internal conflicts are self created because the client holds false or at least unrealistic expectations about someone or something. So much energy is expended in trying to support these expectations that there is little remaining energy available to be used in evaluating alternative possibilities for resolving the

problem. The counseling process frees this psychic energy and allows the client to make responsible (personally acceptable and/or spiritually acceptable) choices and decisions. Such decisions then lead to action, goal setting, and—eventually—to client responsibility for self.

The counselor's role is to aid the client in reducing the conflict or crisis to its narrowest or most critical factors and deal with these one at a time (focusing and structuring). Counselors train clients to use better interpersonal skills in resolving conflicts with others (modeling) and provide a climate in which clients can reach into themselves for the mental, physical, and spiritual resources necessary to resolve the difficulties of life (the creation of trust and hope in the higher self capacities). This is an essential end goal of counseling—otherwise the client will be forever dependent upon the counselor or someone who will serve in the same capacity.

Influencing skills—like all of the skills that we have reviewed—can be weapons or tools in the hands of a counselor. Skills are essential to the counselor's role but they are not magic, nor do they substitute for the selfhood of the counselor as a primary tool by which a client can regain emotional balance and effective, functional discipleship. Influencing is the end result of a well-developed interpersonal relationship constructed by a warm, understanding, and loving counselor. Such a counselor believes in and leads clients to accept their own potentials as persons—persons lovingly and magnificently created and endowed by God to overcome the trials of human existence. When this capability becomes

temporarily lost or hidden, counselors play an influential role in its recovery by offering themselves as "living sacrifices" in time, commitment, caring, authenticity, and trust. These are the personal qualities which inevitably make a counselor "influential" in relating with clients.

PART III

PROFESSIONAL CONCERNS

Chapter 6

AN OVERVIEW OF
COUNSELING THEORIES

INTRODUCTION

A counseling theory is simply a framework or guide from which the counselor approaches the task of counseling. A theory is a rationale for doing what one does in counseling. Your personal approach to counseling should be derived from some consistent personal ideas about values, the nature of humanity, and how behavior is changed. To obtain consistency in your counseling approach requires an understanding of some theoretical foundations used in counseling and psychotherapy.

A large number of counseling theories are used by professional helpers today. Each system, or theory, is based on specific ideas concerning how personality develops, why people behave as they do, and what kinds of methods are required to alleviate problem behaviors. Most of these theories can be broadly grouped into three streams of thought on how a human being should be viewed, psychologically speaking. These three mainstreams of theory—the psychoanalytic force, the behavioral force, and the humanistic force—will be outlined in this chapter. You are urged, however, to take up additional study in at least one of these three broad areas. By doing so, you will become acquainted with additional ideas and methods which you can use to fashion a personal, systematic approach to your own counseling. This, in turn, will contribute to your own confidence and will aid you in your efforts to be a helper to others.

THE PSYCHOANALYTIC VIEW

One of the greatest currents of thought useful to counseling arose from the doctrine and writings of Sigmund Freud during the period 1890-1939. Although some of Freud's later disciples (Jung, Adler, Horney, Sullivan, and others) made modifications to Freud's original ideas, it was Freud himself who produced the first comprehensive "system" of concepts and principles on which much of modern-day therapy is based.

In particular, Freud believed that people are basically evil and are governed by instincts arising out of the unconscious. According to Freud, personal problems today are capable of being linked to early childhood psychosexual concerns and relationships. Early childhood developmental problems are carried over into the relationships established by an individual as an adult.

Among other contributions, Freud outlined three primary levels of personality structure. These were the *id* (responsible for impulsive, pleasure seeking behaviors), the *superego* (a moral or social conscience), and an *ego* (which seeks rational mastery and acts as a "referee" between the id and superego). The conflicts among these various levels of personality structure create a delicate balance for the individual. The human being must defend against both external attack (for yielding to instinctive impulses) and internal disintegration (from conflicting aspects of the personality).

To resolve these conflicts and differences, the individual resorts to defense mechanisms of various types. These are cognitive or physical behavior patterns designed to provide acceptable outlets for the psychic energy created in the unconscious. Often the defense mechanisms serve their purpose. At other times they may become problems in and of themselves—interfering with the individual's daily routine and interactions with others.

Psychoanalytic theory has provided a comprehensive framework for understanding the effects of early childhood experiences and for interpreting the unconscious symbolism in our current behaviors. It has given meaning and focus to the affective aspects of our behaviors. Nevertheless, this viewpoint has some serious limitations. It relegates the individual to a basically evil behavior pattern and a struggle to live with irrational impulses. Furthermore, the idea that a person is controlled by intrapsychic conflicts arising out of past experience often provides an excuse for failure to assume responsibility for one's own life and behavior.

The process of gaining understanding (and thereby personal control) of intrapsychic conflicts is a long and tedious procedure for both a therapist and a client. According to the pure psychoanalytic viewpoint, formal psychoanalysis is required which may take several years of regular appointments with a psychiatrist. However, some psychoanalytic practitioners have more recently introduced short-term dynamic psychotherapy methods which require less time in therapy for carefully selected patients.

Paraprofessional counselors will lack sufficient training to formally use psychoanalytic theory or methodology in dealing with clients. It is helpful, however, to be familiar with some of the basic principles of psychoanalytic theories and to give recognition to the contributions of the unconscious and its effects on our adjustment and behavior.

THE BEHAVIORAL VIEW

From the standpoint of sequential order, behaviorism, or behavioral psychology, is one of the older influences on psychology and the field of counseling. Originating in the late nineteenth century, behaviorism places its emphasis on the objective (that is, observable) aspects of human behavior.

Behavior theory is based on learning principles and the belief that humans, like some other animals, are conditioned to respond to their environment through a sequence of learning experiences. As we react to various stimuli over a lifetime, we build up response patterns. We become creatures of habit. In this sense behaviorism might be viewed as deterministic in that we learn to react in set ways with little aforethought.

In spite of our tendency to develop patterned behavior, as human beings we also possess the capability to reason and understand. This permits us to *relearn*. It is this ability to relearn that constitutes the prime methodology encompassed in behavioral counseling. Little attention is given to the subjective "feelings" of a person. Instead, counseling is viewed as a learning process for the client. Certain desirable behaviors are reinforced positively by the responses, gestures, or other "rewards" managed by the counselor. Behaviors considered undesirable (in the counselor's judgment) are given negative reinforcement (that is, ignored or punished). Operating within these parameters, the counselor attempts to help clients increase self enhancing behaviors and eliminate self defeating or self degrading behaviors. Naturally, this requires considerable knowledge of learning and motivational principles on the part of the counselor.

Behaviorists use performance oriented objectives which require that the counselor must diagnose what behaviors are necessary to solve problem feelings, plan a course of action necessary to teach the client to use such behaviors, and reward intermediate successes en route to meeting the objectives. Similarly, behaviors which interfere with such goals may be extinguished through use of appropriate methodologies. Counseling effectiveness is measured on the basis of whether the desired behaviors are achieved and the behavioral "symptom" is alleviated. The counseling process, then, becomes a "relearning experience" for the client.

Behavioral counseling works best for specific problems which are observable in behavior symptoms. It is often the treatment of choice—when used by a competent mental health practitioner—for such problems as alleviation of fears, overcoming unwanted habits, relieving certain social anxieties, and defeating certain sexual dysfunctions. It does, however, require specific knowledge and training on the part of the counselor.

Opponents of behavioral techniques argue that the dangers of such methods are in the value judgments exercised by the therapist as to what is best for the client. In addition, these opponents argue that the behavioral symptom is not the "real" problem—which exists in the self perceptual or emotional aspects of the client's personality. In actual practice, most behaviorists address the emotional needs of the client through establishment of rapport and by using techniques borrowed from other theories.

THE HUMANISTIC VIEW

The humanistic view, as used here, focuses on the personhood of clients. It is concerned with the uniqueness of the individual and the individuality of each person's perception of reality. Within the broad framework of humanism, we can include *client centered theory* (which focuses on the individual's perception of self), *gestalt theory* (which emphasizes self confrontation in the present time), and *existential theory* (which speaks to individual meaning, purpose, and potential). Humanists, then, are concerned with

1. the capability of the individual to be self aware (the immediacy of *"being"*),
2. the individual's potential (the process of *"becoming,"* or self actualization), and
3. the individual's capability to assume and live by the principle of *rational responsibility* (to take charge of one's own life).

106

These three guidelines provide a framework with which church leaders can be comfortable in their counseling role. As Christians, we are called to be aware of our present state, to fulfill our potential as disciples, and to be responsible in our stewardship. A number of counseling theories lend themselves to this general approach (see preceding paragraph).

One of the best known and most widely researched humanistic approaches is that of *client-centered* counseling, a system of therapy first brought into vogue by Carl R. Rogers *(Client-Centered Therapy)* in 1951. In client-centered counseling, individuals are viewed as being capable of full selfhood unless they are diverted from a normal development pattern. Anxiety is seen as a problem arising out of an incongruence between how the individual views self and the experience of the individual within the environment. To reduce anxiety and psychological conflicts, the client is encouraged to "own" personally held values and to reduce his or her dependence on the expectations and values of others as a guide for living.

Gestalt theory emphasizes self confrontation and living within (becoming aware of) feelings which are current in the immediate moment. Honesty and openness both with self and others is seen as the basic requirement for personal and psychological integration. To obtain this personal honesty and openness, clients are taught to be self aware and to discard phony roles and social games in their interactions with others. A number of techniques for achieving this in counseling have been outlined by Frederick (Fritz) Perls and others *(Gestalt Therapy)*.

107

The issue of rational responsibility for oneself is pursued in a number of counseling theories. *Existentialism* is concerned with people's capabilities to be aware of their personal existence and to fulfill their potential through the process of making rational choices. Anxiety is viewed as the result of avoidance of decision making—thereby creating a purposeless and meaningless existence. Viktor E. Frankl represents one existentialist writer who has written eloquently on the search for personal meaning *(Man's Search for Meaning: An Introduction to Logo-Therapy)*. William Glasser *(Reality Therapy)* and Albert Ellis *(Humanistic Psychotherapy: The Rational-Emotive Approach)* have also outlined counseling theories which approach the issue of self responsibility from the viewpoints of behavior (Glasser) and rational thinking (Ellis).

The humanistic viewpoint has contributed to awareness of the importance of self experience, self perception, and self responsibility. In focusing on such matters, the humanistic theorists have moved counseling and psychotherapy away from tendencies to fit the patient to the therapy. However, they have also opened the floodgates to considerable subjectivity in defining the counseling process—and to some rather mystical endeavors by inadequately trained "helpers."

SUMMARY

Counseling theories might be viewed on a continuum from a behavior modification or training role on one end, through client-centered and various supportive therapies in the middle, to psychoanalytic approaches on the other end. In between, one will encounter a wide variety of "theories." Some of these offer real potential in terms of helping systems. Others are little more than exploitation of a single technique or therapeutic influence.

Some degree of eclecticism in approach is perhaps most widely used by practicing counselors; however, it is important that they fashion a personal framework or conception of the counseling process from which to work. In doing so, they may wish to borrow from various theories those methods with which they personally feel most comfortable.

As indicated in chapter two, it is the relationship developed with the client that is the primary tool of the counselor. Theories are simply systematic approaches used for direction in making the relationship therapeutic in nature. In any theory, the primary focus must be kept on the client as an experiencing, growing person. Only in this way will the helping relationship, and whatever theoretical approach is used, come to its most fruitful conclusion.

Exercise 22: **Select at least one of the books referenced in this chapter and check it out from your local library if available. After reading this book (or an alternate selection on some counseling theory), visit one or more local mental health practitioners (psychiatrist, psychologist, social worker, or mental health counselor) and ask them to explain their theory of counseling. Don't be afraid to ask questions (most mental health professionals love to talk about these ideas).**

CHAPTER 7

CONCLUDING THOUGHTS

HAZARDS IN COUNSELING

In the process of counseling another human being, an authentic, caring relationship is essential. As in all human relationships, the development of a counseling relationship may be hindered by a number of obstacles. Furthermore, even a carefully nurtured therapeutic relationship often contains hazards for the unsuspecting counselor. As counselors we should maintain an awareness of these possible blockages in progress and circumvent them during the counseling process.

We must look first to ourselves for possible problems in counseling. We must avoid playing a "role" of counselor, such as being overeager to be a helper to everyone whether or not we have been asked to help. We must be careful that we do not fall into stereotyped response patterns where "fact finding," "advice giving," or "labeling" become the major ways of responding to clients. A posture of natural, concerned caring and an authentic communication style are sufficient when appropriately used.

The effective counselor also looks to personal values

and cultural biases as possible obstacles or areas of conflict. When we have been reared in and identify with certain groups, values, concepts, and the like, we often tend to adopt rather rigid belief systems. To us, the way we view things is *the* way it is. In such inflexible stances, prejudice, egocentric thinking, and dogmatism can easily find a breeding ground. While it is obvious that there are some universal truths to which we are called to respond, we must also be ready to admit the possibility of changes in what we *personally* may have considered enduring truths. It is always possible that our own human understanding has been limited in some way.

Philosophically, too, we may experience difficulties in our counseling endeavors. Each person usually arrives at some personal ideas or concepts about the basic nature of human beings, how persons develop and grow, the nature of "good" and "bad." We need this framework nailed down for ourselves before attempting to aid our clients in rebuilding their own psychological houses. Of course, it goes without saying that the counselor and client need not have perfectly matched philosophies of life in order for the counseling to be successful.

The value system and typical interaction patterns of the counselor may be hazards in and of themselves. The counselor may, for instance, tend to subtly assume personal responsibility for the client, impose personally owned values on the client, or act in a "parental" manner. This overly protective, dependency creating kind of approach on the counselor's part can be detrimental to the client's successful growth as a person. Yet, because it is so difficult to "see ourselves as others see us," we must be on constant guard that such practices

111

do not gradually creep into our counseling activities.

Clients, too, create a number of possible hazards to the counseling process. Most people are usually somewhat resistant to the idea that they may be in need of counseling assistance. Initially, a client may display defensiveness, false preconceptions about counseling, and a fear of making changes. Often, persons are quite anxious about whether the counseling session content will be kept truly confidential in nature. As these various anxieties are stirred up, a client may make use of disguised defenses such as playing up to the counselor as a "poor me" soul, testing the counselor's personal commitment and values, or attempting to manipulate the counseling process toward previously desired outcomes. All of these ploys can be hazardous to an effective outcome if they are indefinitely left unchallenged by the counselor. A careful mixture of empathy and confrontation is needed by the counselor to dispose of such obstacles.

Finally, emotional or social entanglements between counselor and client should be avoided. The counseling relationship is a powerful one. The client's need to be rescued from crisis and protected from life's difficulties (or so the client perceives) may create an overly dependent relationship which if not carefully monitored by the counselor, can lead to overinvolvement and difficulty in eventually terminating the counseling. A counselor's attempts to be a genuinely warm and caring person may represent interpersonal qualities not present in the client's other relationships. It is the counselor's responsibility to avoid satisfying personal ego needs by playing into the client's temporary need for protection, love, or a permanent supporting helper. The counselor can accomplish this only by maintaining a full understanding of self and self needs, the counseling process and its effects, and a recognition that clients eventually "outgrow" these needs if the pace and tempo of the counseling encounter remain professional in nature and conduct.

MAKING REFERRALS

No counselor can be all things to all people. In spite of the best skills, intentions, and concerns, failures can occur in counseling as frequently as in any other undertaking. Even if counseling appears to have been successful to a given point, a referral may be needed to deal with selected aspects of the problem. At other times the need for referral may become apparent in the first few moments of the first session with a client. When this occurs, you as counselor need to be prepared for taking the appropriate action.

The first issue in referral counseling concerns the question of recognizing those who should be referred. You should normally refer a client who

1. has become too emotionally involved with you—in either a positive or negative way.
2. has tiggered emotional responses in you which will lead to your own overinvolvement with the client (e.g., you have unresolved problems of your own).
3. fails to show signs of being helped by you after a reasonable number of sessions.
4. is psychiatrically disturbed or shows signs of severe mental illness. These may include

(a) strange and abrupt changes in normal behavior patterns.

(b) hearing voices or seeing things which obviously do not or could not exist.

(c) performing repetitive bizarre behaviors or repeatedly thinking strange thoughts.

(d) being unaware of the proper time, location, or of own identity.

(e) beliefs that other persons are out to get him or her or are secretly monitoring his or her activities in some miraculous way.

(f) being greatly withdrawn or unusually hostile or aggressive.

5. may be in need of medical treatment or diagnosis by a physician for some physical ailment.

6. has a specialized problem for which some community agency is especially equipped to provide assistance (e.g., alcoholism or drug treatment, mental retardation, need for institutionalization).

7. indicates severe depression or hints at the possibility of suicide (such clients may need the temporary benefits of psychiatric medicine as well as counseling).

In addition, you may wish to refer any client who for some reason creates a negative reaction in you. Naturally, this cannot be used as an excuse for not wanting to help; however, the client deserves to be referred if you are unable to resolve such feelings.

Referral is the process of aiding a client to move to a more appropriate source for assistance. It may be necessitated by specialized needs, counselor insistence, lack of qualifications on the part of the counselor, or perhaps even incompatibility. If the decision is made by you, a new crisis may be created for the client who may feel rejected or "hopeless" as a result of such a suggestion. Even when clients recognize and agree with the needs for referral, they must still face the necessity of starting over with a new helper in a new setting. This can mean retracing all the information and anxieties raised to that point in the counseling, thus creating discouragement on the part of the client.

In making a referral to another resource agency or person, your first task will be that of helping the client recognize and accept the need for referral. This should be begun as soon as you sense that a referral may be needed. By careful references to the assistance provided by other agencies, without giving the impression of abandoning the client, you can usually "lead" a person to the recognition that more appropriate help can be obtained elsewhere. Certainly, you will continue to maintain a supportive, caring relationship with the client until an agreement for referral is reached.

A second major stumbling block in the referral process is often the counselor's own lack of knowledge regarding appropriate and available helping resources. Without accurate information concerning such resources, and an operable link to them, you will find it difficult indeed to motivate a client to use them! Referral is made much easier if you have developed a number of contacts with other agencies and can place your client in touch with one of these contact persons. Furthermore, by enlarging your network of referral sources and professional counseling "consultants," you will gain valuable information as to the quality of services provided by various persons and agencies in your community. This will help you in making a referral which will actually help your client in a positive way.

Major referral sources with whom you may wish to become acquainted and establish a referral relationship include the following:

1. A psychiatrist. Such practitioners are usually trained in dynamic psychotherapy and, as MDs, can disperse appropriate stabilizing drugs if required.

2. Local mental health center or family guidance agency. Such agencies usually include a wide variety of mental health services including individual, group, and family counseling.

3. Alcoholics Anonymous. This agency is a noted alcoholism rehabilitation support group. A support group for relatives of alcoholics, Al-Anon, also exists. Other drug-related treatment centers and agencies can usually be located through local hospitals, the Council on Chemical Abuse, or under Alcoholism Information or Social Service Agencies in the yellow pages of the telephone directory.

4. Mental health counselors. A listing of Certified Clinical Mental Health Counselors may be obtained from the National Academy of Certified Clinical Mental Health Counselors, 10700 62nd St., Temple Terrace, Florida 33617.

5. Social service agencies. These are normally listed under Social Service Organizations in the yellow pages. While every community is different in

terms of the variety of agencies which are available, such agencies as a twenty-four-hour HELP line, crisis centers for women, Legal Aid, home health services, mental retardation agencies, crisis teams, planned parenthood centers, etc., are usually represented.

6. Private mental health practitioners. These may include psychiatric social workers, psychologists, and others. Many are highly trained and licensed by the state of residence. Many will also be working in local service agencies as well as maintaining private practice hours. You should use such persons only after carefully assessing their qualifications, training, and personal skills. This can be done by a personal visit or inquiring of other persons in the community. Usually a licensed person with a graduate degree in psychology or social work will possess suitable skills for providing sound mental health assistance. Personal competencies, of course, will require verification.

It is your responsibility to be familiar with various community agencies and their services. You must also become as well informed about the quality of services provided as it is possible to do so. When a referral must be made to an agency or person of unknown quality, you should continue some contact with the client until you are assured that the person is, in fact, being adequately served elsewhere. Of course, such continued contact is usually worthwhile in any case, since it proves your support and concern.

117

Once a referral source has been selected and initially approached, you must aid the client in actually seeking help from this source. Generally, it is beneficial if a contact person's name is given to the client and the client encouraged to make the appointment. You can follow up by telephone to determine if an appointment was made or how it went. In cases of extreme reluctance or lack of motivation, you may be required to go with or assist the client in making contact the first time. In either instance, it is your responsibility to make the transition to a new helper as easy as possible. The primary objective is to avoid "losing" the client between the referral and the actual contact with the new assisting agency or person.

Referral is often an integral part of the counseling process. It does not necessarily reflect failure on the part of the counselor. Frequently, a well planned referral is the best indicator of a counselor who is sufficiently intelligent to recognize her/his own limitations or areas of insufficient training. Referrals made under such conditions are certainly in the best interests of a client and represent ethical behavior on the part of the counselor. Also, the client is spared the agony of suffering through a long counseling process which proves, in the end, to be inconclusive in terms of helping improve the client's emotional or behavioral functioning.

Referral is as much a counseling skill as are other skills which go into the counseling process. Unfortunately, it is often treated lightly or neglected by the busy counselor who is just too busy to thoroughly investigate the community network upon which future referral counseling may depend. Every person seeking help from a counselor is entitled to obtain the best possible assistance. The counselor who, for whatever reason, cannot provide this is ethically bound to refer the client elsewhere.

Exercise 23: **Try to make an appointment with at least one psychiatrist, one mental health agency, and one other social service agency. This can usually be done by simply calling and explaining your purpose (information gathering). At each of these scheduled visits, ask what services are provided, what training each therapist has, what professional affiliations are maintained, and, most important, try to make a personal assessment of the person to whom you are speaking. Repeat this exercise twice during the next year with different agencies or persons.**

PERSONAL GROWTH

As you engage in the process of serving as a helper to others in emotional pain, you will soon realize that all of life, including counseling, is a process of growing. As living organisms, we cannot remain the same without stagnation. We must either grow or decline. In truth, we frequently alternate in doing both. The very process of birth itself marks the beginning of an inevitable physical death. Nevertheless, this death will be preceded by tremendous growth before the declining years arrive. We are finding, in fact, that personal and spiritual growth need not be limited to the early developmental, or even middle years, but may be stretched out indefinitely over the life-span.

In this process of growth toward full personal and

spiritual self-realization, one undergoes many "growing pains." Some are self-manufactured; some are externally imposed upon us. Still, many of these trials and crises create opportunities for growth. How we live with and react to such trials often determines the nature and success of our self-growth. A sign recently placed in a local grocery store emphasized this point. It read: "Which One Are You?" Beneath this caption was a raft which simply drifted with the prevailing current, a sailboat which depended upon fickle winds for its speed and direction, and a steamboat which was powered from within. Our role as counselors is to enable people to become powered from within. We grow by being in touch with our personal and spiritual capacities to respond in a positive and responsible way to the challenges of living as human beings. Counseling is a process of helping achieve this state—or re-achieve it—during periods of crisis or concern.

Dr. William C. Menninger, founder of the Menninger Foundation, once outlined the criteria of emotional maturity as follows:

- The ability to deal constructively with reality.
- The capacity to adapt to change.
- A relative freedom from symptoms that are produced by tensions and anxieties.
- The capacity to find more satisfaction in giving than receiving.
- The capacity to sublimate, to direct one's instinctive hostile energy into creative and constructive outlets.
- The capacity to love.

When people can meet these conditions, they will have come a long way toward self responsibility and self management. When we can meet these conditions in our own lives, we will have greatly increased the likelihood of success in our counseling encounters with members of our congregations and others.

Naturally, you cannot stop with this book if you wish to continue to grow as a counselor. It has been designed only as a starting point. An attempt has been made to provide you with a framework of skills and attitudes for making a successful start. To develop artistry in the counseling role, you must continue to grow both in understanding and skills. This can be achieved most effectively through a planned program of self study and actual counseling practice. Personal growth will occur when you resolve to maintain constant self awareness and when you can comfortably accept what you are and how you need to change. Spiritual growth requires a continuing awareness of your unique relationship with God and a fuller development of that relationship through divine-human communication. It also requires an active commitment to place the spiritual self in command of your own self structure system.

In this book, I have attempted to provide a basic foundation. As you choose to experience living, concerned encounters with others, as a helper, you will no doubt discover the agonies and joys of helping another person to grow through effective counseling. It is a role which calls for both personal and spiritual leadership. The authority and competency for this role call for the same qualities which God saw in you when he called you to be a disciple and to occupy a leadership role.

Those qualities need only be enhanced and called forth by your recognition and development of the power that comes from within. For clients and counselors, self and spirit are essential ingredients in spiritual counseling—and in the development of a fully satisfying personhood.

* * *

EPILOGUE

*"There will come a time, I know, when people will take
delight in one another, when each will be a star to the
other, and when each will listen to his fellow as to music.
Then free men will walk with open hearts, and the heart
of each will be pure of envy and greed, and therefore all
mankind will be without malice, and there will be
nothing to divorce the heart from reason. Then life will
be one great service to man! His figure will be raised to
lofty heights—for to free men all heights are attainable.
Then we shall live in truth and freedom and in beauty,
and those will be accounted the best who will the more
widely embrace the world with their hearts, and whose
love of it will be the profoundest; those will be the best
who will be the freest; for in them is the greatest beauty.
Then will life be great and the people will be great who
live that life."*

—Maxim Gorky

*"Then said Jesus to those Jews which believed on him, If
ye continue in my word, then are ye my disciples indeed;
and ye shall know the truth, and the truth shall make you
free."*

—John 8:31, 32.

123

GLOSSARY OF COUNSELING TERMS

— A —

ACTIVATING EVENT: a rational emotive counseling term specifying the event which a client assumes is the cause of a particular emotion.

ADLERIAN THEORY: a theory of personality development and psychotherapy based on the importance of early social and family relationships; developed by Alfred Adler.

ATTENDING (BEHAVIOR): verbal and nonverbal behaviors which demonstrate attentive listening; eye contact, attentive body posture, and verbal following.

ATTITUDE: cognitive posture assumed and reflected in action, feeling, or mood.

AUTHENTICITY: a quality of being one's genuine, real self in relationships with other persons.

AUTHORITY: having the legal or rightful power to act.

— B —

BEHAVIOR THEORY: a theory of personality development and psychotherapy methods centered on observable and measurable behaviors; having to do with learning based on reactions to stimuli under specified conditions.

BODY LANGUAGE: body postures, facial expressions, and similar nonverbal indicators which act as a means of communication.

— C —

CATHARSIS: ventilation or release of emotions and/or accompanying feelings.

CLIENT-CENTERED THEORY: principles of personality development and psychotherapy as developed by Carl Rogers; having to do with the maintenance of a nonjudgmental, positive-regard climate in which a client is free to examine self and the realities of his/her own frame of reference.

CLOSE-ENDED QUESTIONS: questions which are designed to solicit specific information or data; those requiring short answers which do not lend themselves to client exploration or elaboration.

CONCRETENESS: being specific; pinpointing and accurately defining personal feelings and experiences.

CONFRONTATION: the act of challenging the perception of the client; illuminating the incongruity between events, feelings, thoughts, or behaviors.

CONSEQUENCE: a rational emotive counseling term

used to describe the emotion or feeling which results from an individual's rational or irrational belief about an activating event.

COUNSELING: the purposeful and responsible development of an affective-oriented interpersonal relationship which serves as a therapeutic medium for assisting other persons to explore, evaluate, and make changes in their self system in ways which will enhance their personal, social, and spiritual development and adjustment.

— D —

DEEPER FEELINGS: feelings or emotions which underlie a client's surface or readily apparent emotions; may or may not be in the awareness of the client.

DEFENSE MECHANISM: an adopted substitute method or alternative way of handling an emotion or the anxiety accompanying the emotion.

DIRECTIVE: a counselor orientation; having to do with the counselor taking a more active or leading role.

DISPUTING: a rational-emotive term having to do with logically and scientifically attacking irrational beliefs which contribute to unwanted emotions.

— E —

ECLECTICISM: a theory of counseling which makes systematic use of methods and principles from more than one school of thought or theory of counseling.

EMPATHY: understanding and communicating that understanding of another individual; being able to view circumstances from the perspective of another individual as if you were the other person.

ETHICS: moral values and duties; the principles on which one's practice and behaviors are based.

EXISTENTIALISM: a theoretical base which recognizes the "essence of presence" of persons; the acceptance of existence in the immediate moment with choices playing a role in the building of a meaningful existence as a human being.

— F —

FACILITATION: the act of enabling another person to grow; providing opportunities for self enhancing behaviors to occur.

FOCUS: selective attention to specific topics, verbalizations, or feelings expressed by a client; attempting to narrow a client's attention to a selected area or topic.

FREE ASSOCIATION: a psychoanalytic practice of allowing a client to freely verbalize thoughts as they occur, on the assumption that an accumulation of such thoughts will reveal the nature and causes of the client's disturbance.

— G —

GENUINENESS: being "real" or honest with others; personal transparency; avoidance of role playing when interacting with others.

— H —

HIDDEN SELF: aspects of the self system which one either does not accept or wishes to hide from the knowledge of other persons.

HOMEWORK: a behavioral term used to describe between-session assignments given to a client in order to practice or reinforce positive behaviors or more responsible approaches to thinking and/or behavior.

HUMANISTIC THEORY: a broad term encompassing counseling theories which view human beings as in the process of becoming; a view which espouses the uniqueness and potential of the individual.

— I —

IDEAL STEP: a self constructed image of "how I want to be"; often based on unrealistic expectations or on adopted standards which are external to the individual's own true value systems.

IMMEDIACY: concentration on the current "here-and-now" aspects of the counseling process; focusing on the immediate experiences of the two participants.

INFERIORITY: actual or imagined lack of equality with others in some sphere of living or behavior.

INSIGHT: discernment or understanding of; awareness or immediate cognition of a phenomenon not previously understood or recognized.

INTERPRETATION: to explain, construct, or provide the meaning of something drawn together by the observer.

— J —

JOHARI WINDOW: a graphic model depicting self aspects related to self disclosure and interpersonal communication.

— L —

LISTENING: giving full attention to; a group of trained responses which demonstrate active attention to and hearing of another person.

— M —

MINIMAL ENCOURAGEMENT RESPONSE: a neutral verbalization or nonverbal indicator which encourages a client to continue talking.

— N —

NEEDS: internal or external factors or desires which motivate or stimulate the organism to act in specified ways to achieve satisfaction. Lower order needs (existence needs) must be satisfied before higher order needs (self actualizing needs) will be acted upon.

NONDIRECTIVE: pertaining to a group of counseling behaviors or methods oriented toward a passive or following role on the part of the counselor; an attempt to stimulate the client to explore and arrive at self determined decisions.

129

— O —

OPEN-ENDED QUESTIONS: questions which are designed to encourage elaboration by the client; usually beginning with "would," "could," or "how."

OPENNESS: a quality of interpersonal interaction which demonstrates willingness to portray one's true attitudes and feelings.

— P —

PARAPHRASING: "feeding back" to the client what he/she has said, but in your own words; a verbal method of assuring accurate understanding of what the client has expressed.

PARROTING: responding by restating *exactly* how the client expressed a feeling, as opposed to how you felt he/she experienced it.

PSYCHOANALYTIC THEORY: a system of personality development and psychotherapy principles founded on the work of Sigmund Freud; having to do with the relation of current problems to problems which occurred in the psychosexual history of the individual.

PSYCHOPATHOLOGY: the scientific study of mental disorders as viewed from a psychological point of view; also, a state of behavior clinically determined as deviating from the norm to a sufficient degree as to be identifiable as a pattern of behavior or syndrome which fits a classification of mental disorder.

PSYCHOTHERAPY: the mental treatment of illness, especially nervous diseases or maladjustments, by psychoanalysis, reeducation, or scientific method of relearning or behavior alteration; closely related to clinical counseling in methodology (see *Counseling*) but also differing in some dimensions according to various theorists.

— R —

RAPPORT: a climate of mutual trust and respect between persons; a workable relationship.

RATIONAL EMOTIVE THEORY (RET): a theory of emotional causation and control espoused by Albert Ellis; principles based on the belief that the person's expectations or faulty thinking processes are responsible for emotional disturbances.

REALITY THEORY: a body of psychotherapy or counseling principles espoused by William Glasser; based on the belief that emotional health is based on responsible behaviors and a feeling of success.

REFERRAL (PROCESS): the act of turning a client over to another person or agency for assistance either supplementary to or in lieu of one's own efforts.

REFLECTING: responding in a manner which feeds back what another person has expressed or felt.

REINFORCEMENT: reward or act designed to encourage the repetition of a specific behavior or response.

RESPONDING: reacting to another person or situation in a manner which demonstrates presence (effective responding).

RESPONSIBILITY: state or quality of being accountable; an assumed requirement of effective emotional functioning.

— S —

SELF ACCEPTANCE: the difference between self concept and ideal self images; the degree to which the individual recognizes and "owns" the current status of the self structure system which is hers or his.

SELF ACTUALIZATION: the process of becoming all that one has the potential to become; a state of being in which one would have achieved a number of personal qualities and behaviors as outlined by psychologist Abraham Maslow. In terms of spiritual growth, such a state would be represented by a fully functional higher self rendering a full stewardship.

SELF AWARENESS: being cognizant of aspects of the self structure system which contribute to images of self.

SELF CONCEPT: a self structure system image of "how I am"; an individual's current psychological awareness or perception of self.

SELF DISCLOSURE: an interpersonal response which reveals some personal aspect of self. Counselor's attempt to self disclose in ways which are both timely and appropriate to the current discussion.

SELF ESTEEM: the degree to which an individual accepts himself/herself in a positive way.

SELF IDEAL: see *Ideal Self.*

SELF SYSTEM: a psychological construct consisting of

a variety of internalized images which make up the personhood of the individual; a cognitive apparition useful in explaining selfhood.

SPIRITUAL SELF: an individually unique combination of spirit in interaction with learned values, experiences with God, spiritually significant others, and personal practices; the Creator-inspired aspect of the self system.

STRUCTURING: a progressive ordering of material being discussed in counseling. See also *Focus*.

SUMMARIZING: the drawing together of various topics and feelings expressed by a client into a unified or clarified whole for further discussion.

SURFACE FEELINGS: superficial and/or readily apparent feelings held by the client.

— T —

TASK SKILLS: specific behaviors and ways of communicating or being which are modeled by the counselor and learned by the client in order to further the counseling process and increase the client's ability to be self directing and self responsible.

TRANSFERENCE: a psychoanalytic term having to do with the direction of feelings and desires, retained unconsciously from childhood, to new objects.

TRIANGLE OF TRUST: a term constructed by the author to project the importance of using empathy, warmth, and respect in a balanced way in order to build trust in a counseling relationship.

TRUST: assured reliance on another's integrity; a shared confidence and hope; an essential foundation for the development of a successful counseling encounter.

— U —

UNCONDITIONAL POSITIVE REGARD: a full acceptance and appreciation of the client as a person (although not necessarily of the client's behaviors).
UNDERSTANDING: discerning and comprehending; fully knowing.

— V —

VALUES: core beliefs which are held in high esteem, chosen freely from among alternatives, prized, publicly affirmed, and repeatedly acted upon.

— W —

WARMTH: a genuine caring and concern for another person; expressed love in a Christian sense.

BIBLIOGRAPHY

Brammer, Lawrence M. *The Helping Relationship: Process and Skills* (New Jersey: Prentice-Hall, Inc., 1973).

Carkhuff, Robert R. *Helping and Human Relations: A Primer for Lay and Professional Helpers* (New York: Holt, Rinehart and Winston, Inc., 1969).

Carkhuff, Robert R., and Berenson, B. G. *Beyond Counseling and Therapy* (New York: Holt, Rinehart and Winston, Inc., 1967, 1977).

Corsini, Raymond (Editor). *Current Psychotherapies* (Itasca, Illinois: F. E. Peacock Publishers, Inc., 1973).

Danish, Steven J., and Hauer, Allen L. *Helping Skills: A Basic Training Program* (New York: Human Sciences Press, 1973).

Egan, Gerard. *Interpersonal Living* (Monterey, California: Brooks/Cole Publishing Co., 1976).

Ellis, Albert. *Humanistic Psychotherapy the Rational Emotive Approach* (New York: The Julian Press, Inc., 1973).

Frankl, Viktor E. *Man's Search for Meaning: An Introduction to Logotherapy* (Boston: Beacon Press, 1962).

Gazda, George M., and Asbury, Frank R., and Balzar, Fred J., and Childers, William C., and Walters, Richard P. *Human Relations Development, A Manual for Educators* (Boston: Allyn & Bacon, Inc., 1977).

Glasser, William. *Reality Therapy* (New York: Harper and Row, 1965).

Ivey, Allen E., and Gluckstern, Norma B. *Basic Attending Skills and Basic Influencing Skills*, Participant Manuals (North Amherst, Massachusetts: Microtraining Associates, Inc., 1976).